本教材受教育部中外语言交流合作中心 2020 年国际中文教育重点项目
"国际中文教育教材的研发和课程建设"资助

我是医学生
I Am a Medical Student

基础医学汉语 课本 1
Preclinical Medicine Chinese Textbook 1

总 主 编：朱瑞蕾　甄　珍
本册主编：张杏春
副 主 编：张举英　甄　珍
编　　者：张杏春　甄　珍　张举英　李晓婧　朱瑞蕾

北京语言大学出版社
BEIJING LANGUAGE AND CULTURE UNIVERSITY PRESS

©2022 北京语言大学出版社，社图号 22049

图书在版编目（CIP）数据

我是医学生. 基础医学汉语. 1. 课本 / 朱瑞蕾，甄珍总主编；张杏春分册主编. —北京：北京语言大学出版社，2022.8（2025.3重印）
ISBN 978-7-5619-6110-0

Ⅰ. ①我… Ⅱ. ①朱… ②甄… ③张… Ⅲ. ①医学—汉语—对外汉语教学—教材 Ⅳ. ①H195.4

中国版本图书馆CIP数据核字（2022）第101457号

我是医学生：基础医学汉语　课本1
WO SHI YIXUESHENG：JICHU YIXUE HANYU　KEBEN 1

排版制作：	华伦图文制作中心
责任印制：	邝　天

出版发行：	北京语言大学出版社	
社　　址：	北京市海淀区学院路15号，100083	
网　　址：	www.blcup.com	
电子信箱：	service@blcup.com	
电　　话：	编辑部	8610-82303395
	发行部	8610-82303650/3591/3648
	北语书店	8610-82303653
	网购咨询	8610-82303908
印　　刷：	北京富资园科技发展有限公司	

版　次：	2022年8月第1版		印　次：	2025年3月第3次印刷
开　本：	787毫米×1092毫米　1/16		印　张：	16.25
字　数：	211千字			
定　价：	78.00元			

PRINTED IN CHINA
凡有印装质量问题，本社负责调换. 售后QQ号1367565611，电话010-82303590

前 言

《我是医学生：基础医学汉语》系列教材是一套在"中文＋医学"理念指导下，依据《新汉语水平考试大纲》《国际中文教育中文水平等级标准》《医学汉语水平考试（MCT）大纲》编写的综合性医学专用汉语教材。教材重在提高学习者在日常生活交际和医院日常交际场景中运用汉语的能力，同时也注重提升学习者的文化素养和医生职业素质。

本套教材主要适用于来华学习基础医学专业的汉语零起点医学生，同时也适用于：（1）来华学习临床医学专业的医学生；（2）来华学习中医学专业的医学生；（3）来华工作的医学专家及短期研修的医学生；（4）有汉语学习需求的海外医学生。

一、编写理念

本套教材将医学专业汉语学习者的日常汉语学习和HSK应考能力提高相结合，将医学专业知识和社会文化知识相结合，以实现汉语、医学和文化相互融合的编写目标。本套教材从零起点开始培养学习者的听、说、读、写技能，帮助学习者逐步掌握HSK一至四级所规定的词汇、语言点和话题任务，熟悉《医学汉语水平考试（MCT）大纲》所规定的医学专业词汇、话题和任务，提高在日常生活交际和医院日常交际场景中运用汉语的能力，同时通过汉语学习了解医生的职业特点，感受"医者仁心""医德为先"的高尚情操。

二、教材架构

《我是医学生：基础医学汉语》系列教材包括课本4册、配套练习册4册，每册15课。具体安排如下：

第1册侧重汉语日常交际能力的培养，适度增加简单的医学场景交流。其中，正课前的"汉语拼音"和"拼音练习"部分对现代汉语语音知识进行了集中的讲授和练习，后面的1—5课也对其不断进行复现和强化。完成第1册的学习，学习者汉语水平可以达到HSK二级，能够熟悉常用的医学专业词汇，并进行简单的医学场景交流。

第2册将汉语日常交际能力的培养与医学场景中交流能力的提升相结合，所涉及的交际场景更加多样，交流范围更加广阔，所反映的中国社会文化也更加丰富。完成第2册的学习，学习者汉语水平可以达到HSK三级，医学专业词汇进一步增加，并能进行常见的医学场景交流。

第3册和第4册进一步拓展汉语日常交际的广度和深度，日常交际任务更加丰富；所涉医学场景更加侧重医院常见科室的寻医问诊，医患交流场景更加具体、真实，多是通过专科医生了解常见疾病的症状和治疗方案。完成第3册和第4册的学习，学习者汉语水平可以达到甚至超过HSK四级，能够掌握常用的医学专业词汇，了解常见疾病的基本知识，感受医生的职业特点和高尚情操。

三、教材特点

1. 汉语、医学和文化相互融合

《我是医学生：基础医学汉语》系列教材的编写目标包括汉语、医学和文化三个方面。汉语目标是核心目标，主要包括汉语知识目标和汉语技能目标，是实现医学目标和文化目标的基础。本套教材是医学专用汉语教材，医学目标包括医学词汇目标、医学场景交流目标和医学文化目标，主要通过营造医学场景的方式实现。文化目标包括知识文化目标和交际文化目标，本套教材致力于加深学习者对中国社会文化的了解，提高学习者的跨文化交际能力，促进学习者对多元文化的理解。文化目标的实现依赖于语言教学内容中具体文化目标的完成。汉语目标和文化目标属于中文目标，医学目标属于专业目标，三者完美融合于本套教材中。

2. 听、说、读、写并重

本套教材是综合性医学专用汉语教材，在语言技能培养方面，听、说、读、写并重。每篇课文后的"综合练习"部分针对重点词汇、语法、汉字、句型和课文内容进行反复练习，巩固学习者的语言知识；每课后的"语言任务"部分针对口头表达和书面表达能力设计输出型语言任务，重在培养学习者的语言产出能力。配套练习册除进一步巩固汉语重点知识、强化重点能力培养外，还通过丰富的练习题型，训练学习者解决各种语言问题的应用能力，提高HSK应考能力。

3. 通用和专用大纲兼顾

通用汉语词汇、语言点和话题任务重点参照《新汉语水平考试大纲》，同时参照《国际中文教育中文水平等级标准》，医学专业词汇、话题和任务重点参照《医学汉语水平考试（MCT）大纲》。本套教材覆盖《新汉语水平考试大纲》一至四级全部词汇、语言点和话题任务，同时覆盖《医学汉语水平考试（MCT）大纲》一至三级全部话题和任务，以及大部分词汇。

4. 依据试用反馈不断调整完善

本套教材在山东大学临床医学专业（外国留学生）已进行了三轮试用，每次试用后我们都会进行教学效果和学生需求的实证研究与分析，根据教师教学反馈和学生学习反馈进行调整和修改。教材试用结果表明，本套教材可以有效满足医学相关专业学生日常交流、临床实习、通过HSK四级考试和了解中国社会文化的需要。

除此之外，本套教材还在江西中医药大学试用了一个学期，在美国阿拉巴马大学（University of Alabama）试用了两个学期，都取得了显著的教学效果，我们根据试用反馈进行了进一步的调整和修改。

四、编写体例

根据语言学习规律和医学能力培养规律，本套教材各册的编写体例略有差异，具体如下：

1. 第1册编写体例

◎课本

《课本1》开篇便针对现代汉语语音基础知识进行了集中的讲授和练习，并在后面的1—5课中不断复现和强化。1—15课每课均由学习目标、热身活动、课文与生词、语言点讲解与操练、综合练习、语言任务六部分组成。

学习目标：根据课文内容设置语言功能和语言点目标，帮助学习者了解本课的学习重点。鉴于学习者为零起点的外国留学生，本部分以英文形式呈现。

热身活动：设置两个问题，引入本课主题，激发学习者对学习内容的兴趣，激活学习者已有的背景知识和相关词汇。问题围绕日常交际话题设计。

课文与生词：每课包含两篇课文，课文（一）和课文（二）均为对话体，以医学生的日常交际话题为主，后期逐渐增加医学场景的交际话题。两篇课文之间注重内容的关联和生词、语法的复现。生词紧扣《新汉语水平考试大纲》和《医学汉语水平考试（MCT）大纲》。

语言点讲解与操练：语言点讲解简洁清晰，例句典型而丰富，同时突出语法格式的归纳、易错点的提醒及近义词的辨析。每个语言点后均配有针对性练习。

综合练习：课文（一）和课文（二）后均有紧扣课文内容和知识能力培养的综合练习，前5课主要以"听录音，选出你听到的音节""根据汉字写拼音""朗读语句""完成对话"和"汉字书写"为主，后10课主要以"根据汉字写拼音""朗读语句""替换练习""选词填空""根据课文内容回答问题""根据课文内容填空"和"汉字书写"为主。

语言任务：以现实情景为场景，引导学生完成综合性语言任务，主要包括"阅读理解"和"口头表达"。语言任务以日常交际情景为主，以医学情景为辅。

◎练习册

第1—5课所学习的词汇、语言点和课文相对简单，我们将之融入第6—15

课的练习中。

第6—15课每课包括听力、阅读和书写三个部分。听力部分的练习包括"看图片，听词语，判断对（√）错（×）""看图片，听句子，判断对（√）错（×）"和"听对话，选择正确答案"，阅读部分的练习包括"看图片，并将图片序号填在相关句子后""选词填空"和"选出下列词语在句子中的位置"，书写部分的练习包括"读句子，根据拼音写汉字"和"组词成句"。

2. 第2册编写体例

◎课本

《课本2》每课均由学习目标、热身活动、课文与生词、语言点讲解与操练、综合练习、语言任务、补充词汇七部分组成。

学习目标：根据课文内容设置语言功能、语言点、医学知识和社会文化目标，帮助学习者了解本课的学习重点。同样，鉴于学习者汉语水平较低，本部分以英文形式呈现。

热身活动：设置两个问题，引入本课主题，激发学习者对学习内容的兴趣，激活学习者已有的背景知识和相关词汇。问题主要围绕日常交际话题和医学话题设计。

课文与生词：每课包含两篇课文，课文（一）和课文（二）均为对话体，以医学生的日常交际话题为主，后期逐渐增加医学场景的交际话题。两篇课文之间注重内容的关联和生词、语法的复现。生词紧扣《新汉语水平考试大纲》和《医学汉语水平考试（MCT）大纲》。

语言点讲解与操练：语言点讲解简洁清晰，例句典型而丰富，突出语法格式的归纳、易错点的提醒及近义词的辨析。每个语言点后均配有针对性练习。

综合练习：课文（一）和课文（二）后均有紧扣课文内容和知识能力培养的综合练习，题型主要包括"根据拼音写汉字""辨字组词""替换练习""选词填空""用所给词语完成对话""根据课文内容回答问题"和"根据课文内容填空"。

语言任务：以现实情景为场景，引导学生完成综合性语言任务，主要包括"阅读理解""口头表达"和"书面表达"。语言任务以日常交际情景为主，以医学情景为辅。

补充词汇：补充与本课内容密切相关的医学专业词汇，每课补充4—6个词，每个词均配有拼音、英文翻译和图片。

◎练习册

《练习册2》每课包括听力、阅读和书写三个部分。听力部分的练习包括"听句子，判断对（√）错（×）""听对话，选择正确答案"和"听句子，写下你听到的话"，阅读部分的练习包括"选词填空""选出下列词语在句子中的位置"和"阅读语句，选择正确答案"，书写部分的练习包括"读句子，根据拼音写汉字"和"组词成句"。

3. 第3、4册编写体例

◎课本

《课本3》和《课本4》每课均由学习目标、热身活动、课文与生词、语言点讲解与操练、综合练习、语言任务六部分组成。

学习目标：根据课文内容设置语言功能、语言点、医学知识和社会文化目标，帮助学习者了解本课的学习重点。随着学习者汉语水平的提高，本部分的呈现形式过渡为中文。

热身活动：设置两个问题，引入本课主题，激发学习者对学习内容的兴趣，激活学习者已有的背景知识和相关词汇。问题主要围绕日常交际话题和医学话题设计。

课文与生词：每课包含三篇课文，课文（一）为医学场景对话，课文（二）为日常交流对话，课文（三）为叙述体，其中《课本3》以日常交际话题的叙述为主，《课本4》以医学话题的叙述为主。三篇课文之间注重内容的关联和生词、语法的复现。生词紧扣《新汉语水平考试大纲》和《医学汉语水平考试（MCT）大纲》。

语言点讲解与操练：语言点讲解简洁清晰，例句典型而丰富，突出语法格式的归纳、易错点的提醒及近义词的辨析。每个语言点后均配有针对性练习。

综合练习：课文（一）、课文（二）和课文（三）后均有紧扣课文内容和知识能力培养的综合练习，题型主要包括"根据拼音写汉字""辨字组词""选词填空""选出下列词语在句子中的位置""用所给词语完成对话""根据课文内容回答问题"和"根据课文内容填空"。

语言任务：以现实情景为场景，引导学生完成综合性语言任务，主要包括"阅读理解""口头表达"和"书面表达"。语言任务以医学情景为主。

◎练习册

《练习册3》和《练习册4》每课包括听力、阅读和书写三个部分。听力部分的练习包括"听句子，判断对错"和"听对话，选择正确答案"，阅读部分的练习包括"选择正确的上下文填空""选词填空""排列顺序"和"阅读语段，选择正确答案"，书写部分的练习包括"组词成句""读句子，根据拼音写汉字"和"看图片，用词造句"。

五、教学建议

本套教材建议每课用6—8课时完成。若一周8课时，一学期16周，每学期可完成1册。若选择"主讲＋复练"的教学模式，主讲教师负责教授每课的课文、生词和语言点，并带领学生完成课文后相应的综合练习；复练教师负责生词与语言点的扩展性和交际性练习，并带领学生完成每课的语言任务和练习册上的练习。

六、编写团队

本套教材由长期从事一线医学汉语教学工作的教师编写，总主编为朱瑞蕾、甄珍。

《课本1》和《练习册1》由张杏春、甄珍、张举英、李晓婧、朱瑞蕾编写，张杏春负责统稿。

《课本2》和《练习册2》由张举英、张杏春、李晓婧、朱瑞蕾、甄珍、张海萍、李婷玉编写，张举英负责统稿。

《课本3》和《练习册3》由甄珍、朱瑞蕾、李晓婧、张举英、张杏春编写，甄珍负责统稿。

《课本4》和《练习册4》由李晓婧、朱瑞蕾、甄珍、张举英、张杏春编写，李晓婧负责统稿。

七、鸣谢

本套教材由张杏春、朱瑞蕾、戴丽华、周汶霏、校潇、张云、蔡燕等任课教师在山东大学进行了三个学期的课堂试用，由张海萍、李婷玉在江西中医药大学进行了一个学期的课堂试用，由马玲在美国阿拉巴马大学进行了两个学期的课堂试用，她们都对教材提出了很多切实的修改意见，在此特别致谢！

在教材编写过程中，山东大学李安老师在词频统计方面提供了强大的技术支持，山东大学陈蒙老师在医学词汇选取方面与《医学汉语水平考试（MCT）大纲》进行了严格的对标（参见书后《全四册覆盖MCT大纲词汇表》[①]），李静茹、徐紫钰、温璐妃、刘晓洁、齐梓君、张铭心、曾哲宇等同学在语料整理方面提供了周到的帮助，济南市第二人民医院王旭医师、济南市妇幼保健院侯艳梅医师在医学专业知识和方法方面提供了有力的支持，在此一并感谢。

除此之外，我们还要感谢北京语言大学出版社责任编辑李非飞老师对本套教材提出的宝贵修改意见。

编写团队
2022年4月

[①] 本成果受教育部中外语言交流合作中心2021年国际中文教育研究青年项目"基于需求分析和文本分析的来华预科生医学汉语教材建设研究"（21YH72D）资助。

Foreword

Under the guidance of the concept of "Chinese + medicine", *I Am a Medical Student: Preclinical Medicine Chinese* is a series of integrated medical Chinese textbooks compiled based on *Chinese Proficiency Test Syllabus*, *Chinese Proficiency Grading Standards for International Chinese Language Education* and *Medical Chinese Test (MCT) Syllabus*. The teaching materials focus on improving the learners' ability to use Chinese for communication in daily life and in the hospital, and also focus on improving the learners' cultural literacy and professional quality as doctors.

This series of textbooks is suitable for international preclinical medical students who are the very beginners of Chinese language. It is also suitable for: (1) medical students who come to China to study clinical medicine; (2) medical students who come to China to study traditional Chinese medicine; (3) medical experts working in China and medical students taking short-term training courses; (4) international medical students with the need of learning Chinese.

1. Writing Principles

This series of textbooks combines medical Chinese students' learning of daily Chinese with their improvement of HSK test-taking ability, and combines their medical knowledge with social and cultural knowledge, so as to achieve the integration of Chinese, medicine and culture. This series of textbooks promotes beginners' listening, speaking, reading and writing skills from scratch, helps them gradually master the vocabulary, language points, topics, and tasks stipulated in HSK Levels 1 to 4, and acquaints themselves with the medical vocabulary, topics and tasks stipulated in the *Medical Chinese Test (MCT) Syllabus*. It improves students' ability to use Chinese for communication in daily life and in the hospital, helping them understand the professional characteristics of doctors using Chinese language, and feel the nobility of a doctor's benevolence and medical morality.

2. Textbook Structure

This series of integrated medical Chinese textbooks includes 4 volumes, each consisting of a textbook and the corresponding workbook. Each volume has 15 lessons. The specific arrangements are as follows:

Volume 1 focuses on the cultivation of daily communicative competence in Chinese, moderately increases communication in simple medical scenarios. The "Chinese Pinyin" and "Pinyin exercises" parts before the lessons teach and practice modern Chinese phonetics, which are repeated and strengthened in the following Lessons 1-5. After studying Volume 1, beginners' Chinese proficiency can reach HSK Level 2. They will be familiar with common medical Chinese vocabulary, and communicate in simple medical scenarios.

Volume 2 combines the development of communication skills in daily life with the improvement of communication skills in medical scenarios. The communication scenarios involved are more diverse, the scope of communication is broader, and the Chinese society and culture reflected are also richer. After studying Volume 2, learners' Chinese proficiency can reach HSK Level 3. Learners will further improve their vocabulary in medical Chinese, and they can communicate in common medical scenarios.

Volumes 3 and 4 further expand the breadth and depth of daily communication in Chinese, and the daily communication tasks are richer; the medical scenarios involved more focused on seeing patients in common departments in hospitals, and the doctor-patient communication scenarios more specific and real, most of which are about learning symptoms and specialists' treatment protocols for common diseases. After studying Volumes 3 and 4, learner's Chinese proficiency can reach or even exceed HSK Level 4. They can master common medical Chinese vocabulary, learn the basics of common diseases, and feel the professional characteristics and noble sentiments of doctors.

3. Characteristics of the Textbooks

(1) Integrating Chinese, medicine and culture

The compilation targets of this series of textbooks include three aspects: Chinese, medicine and culture. Learning Chinese is the core target, mainly including learning Chinese knowledge and skills, which is the basis of learning medicine and culture. These are specialized medical Chinese textbooks. The medical targets mainly include learning medical vocabulary, communication in medical scenes, and medical culture, which are mainly achieved by creating medical scenes. Cultural targets include learning knowledge about culture and communication. These textbooks are committed to enhancing students' understanding of Chinese society and culture, improving their cross-cultural communication skills, and promoting their understanding of multiculturalism. The realization of cultural targets depends on the completion of specific cultural targets in language teaching. Learning Chinese language and culture realizes the language target, and learning medicine realizes the professional target. These three are integrated in these textbooks.

(2) Putting equal emphasis on listening, speaking, reading and writing

This is a series of integrated medical specialized Chinese textbook. In terms of the development of language skills, equal emphasis is put on listening, speaking, reading and writing. The "Comprehensive Exercises" part of the textbooks focuses on repetition drills on major vocabulary, grammar points, Chinese characters, sentence patterns and texts to consolidate learners' mastery of language; at the same time, the "Language Tasks" part after each lesson also designs language output tasks to practice language orally and in written forms, focusing on cultivating learners' language production ability. In addition to further consolidating learners' essential knowledge of Chinese and enhancing their development of primary abilities, the accompanying workbooks of the textbooks also train learners' ability to solve various language problems and improve their ability to take the HSK test through a variety of exercises.

(3) Giving consideration to both general and specific syllabuses

For general Chinese vocabulary, language points, topics and tasks, this series of textbooks is based on *Chinese Proficiency Test Syllabus* and *Chinese Proficiency Grading Standards for International Chinese Language Education*. For medical Chinese vocabulary, topics and tasks, this series of textbooks refers to *Medical Chinese Test (MCT) Syllabus*. This series of textbooks covers all the vocabulary, language points, topics, and tasks at Level 1 to Level 4 in *Chinese Proficiency Test Syllabus* and all the topics, tasks and most of the vocabulary at Level 1 to Level 3 in *Medical Chinese Test (MCT) Syllabus*.

(4) Making continuous adjustment and improvement based on the feedback from the trial

This series of textbooks has been used for three rounds in clinical medicine major (for international students) of Shandong University. After each trial, empirical research and analysis on the teaching effect and students' needs were conducted, and adjustments and revisions were made according to the teaching and learning feedback. The trail use of this series of textbooks showed that it can effectively meet medical students' need for daily communication, clinical practice, passing HSK Level 4 and understanding Chinese society and culture.

In addition, this series of textbooks has been tried out for one semester at Jiangxi University of Chinese Medicine and two semesters at the University of Alabama in the United States, both of which have achieved remarkable teaching effects, and we have made further adjustments and revisions based on the trial feedback.

4. Compilation Layout

Following the law of language learning and medical competence development, this series of textbooks is slightly different in the compilation layout of each volume. The specific compilation layouts are as follows:

(1) The compilation layout of Volume 1

◎ Textbook

Textbook 1 teaches and practices the basics of modern Chinese phonetics and recurs and strengthens in Lessons 1 to 5. Each of Lessons 1 to 15 consists of six parts: learning objectives, warm-up, texts and new words, language points explanation and practice, comprehensive exercises, and language tasks.

Learning objectives: Design the language functions and language points based on the text to help learners understand the learning focus of each lesson. Since the learners are beginner-level foreigners, this part is presented in English.

Warm-up: Ask two questions to introduce the theme of the lesson, stimulate learners' interest in the content, and activate the background knowledge and related vocabulary they already acquired. The questions are on topics in daily communication.

Texts and new words: Each lesson includes two texts. Both Text 1 and Text 2 are conversational, focusing on the topics in medical students' daily communication and gradually discussing those in medical scenes. The correlation between the two texts and the recurrence of new words and grammar are emphasized. The new words are based on *Chinese Proficiency Test Syllabus* and *Medical Chinese Test (MCT) Syllabus*.

Language points explanation and practice: Language points are explained concisely and clearly using typical and abundant example sentences. Meanwhile, it highlights the summary of grammar points, the reminders of error-prone points, and the differentiation of synonyms. Each language point comes with targeted exercises.

Comprehensive exercises: After Text 1 and Text 2, there are comprehensive exercises based on the texts and the development of knowledge and ability. The first 5 lessons ask students to "listen to the recording and pick out the syllables you hear", "write Pinyin according to Chinese characters", "read aloud", "complete dialogues", and "write Chinese characters". And the following 10 lessons ask students to "write Pinyin according to Chinese characters", "read aloud", "substitution drills", "use the following words to fill in the blanks", "answer the following questions according to the text", "fill in the blanks according to the text", and "write Chinese characters".

Language tasks: This part takes real-life situations as scenarios and guides students to complete comprehensive language tasks, such as "reading comprehension" and "oral expression". Most language tasks are based on daily communication situations, supplemented by those based on medical situations.

◎ Workbook

The vocabulary, language points and texts in Lessons 1 to 5 are relatively easy, and thus are incorporated into the exercises in Lessons 6 to 15.

Each of Lessons 6 to 15 consists of three parts: listening, reading and writing. The listening exercises include to "look at the pictures, listen to the words and judge right (√) or wrong (×)", "look at the pictures, listen to the sentences and judge right (√) or wrong (×)", and "listen to the dialogues and choose the correct answers". The reading exercises include to "look at the pictures and fill in the picture numbers after the relevant sentences", "use the following words to fill in the blanks", and "choose the correct position of the following words in the sentences". The writing exercises include to "read the following sentences and write Chinese characters according to Pinyin" and "group the following words into sentences".

(2) The compilation layout of Volume 2

◎ Textbook

Each lesson consists of seven parts: learning objectives, warm-up, texts and new words, language points explanation and practice, comprehensive exercises, language tasks, and supplementary vocabulary.

Learning objectives: Design the language functions, language points, medical knowledge, and social culture based on the text to help learners understand the learning focus of each lesson. Since the learners are at the novice level, this part is also presented in English.

Warm-up: Ask two questions to introduce the theme of the lesson, stimulate learners' interest in the content, and activate the background knowledge and related vocabulary they already acquired. The questions are on topics in daily communication and medicine.

Texts and new words: Each lesson includes two texts. Both Text 1 and Text 2 are conversational, focusing on the topics in medical students' daily communication and gradually discussing those in medical scenes. The correlation between the two texts and the recurrence of new words and grammar are emphasized. The new words are based on *Chinese Proficiency Test Syllabus* and *Medical Chinese Test (MCT) Syllabus*.

Language points explanation and practice: Language points are explained concisely and clearly using typical and abundant example sentences. Meanwhile, it highlights the summary of grammar points, the reminders of error-prone points, and the differentiation of synonyms. Each language point comes with targeted exercises.

Comprehensive exercises: After Text 1 and Text 2, there are comprehensive exercises based on the texts and the development of knowledge and ability. The types of questions mainly include to "write Chinese characters according to Pinyin", "discriminate between Chinese characters and make words", "substitution drills", "use the following words to fill in the blanks", "complete the dialogues with given words", "answer the following questions according to the text", and "fill in the blanks according to the text".

Language tasks: This part takes real-like situations as scenarios and guides students to complete comprehensive language tasks, such as "reading comprehension", "oral expression" and "written expression". Most language tasks are based on daily communication situations, supplemented by those based on medical situations.

Supplementary vocabulary: It supplements medical vocabulary closely related to this lesson. Each lesson is supplemented with 4-6 words with Pinyin, English translations and pictures.

◎ Workbook

Each lesson consists of three parts: listening, reading and writing. The listening exercises include to "listen to sentences and judge right (√) or wrong (×)", "listen to dialogues and choose the correct answers", and "listen to sentences and write down what you heard". The reading exercises include to "use the following words to fill in the blanks", "choose the correct positions of the following words in the sentences", and "read the following sentences and choose the correct answers". The writing exercises include to "read the following sentences and write Chinese characters according to Pinyin" and "group the following words into sentences".

(3) The compilation layout of Volumes 3 and 4

◎ Textbooks

Each lesson consists of six parts: learning objectives, warm-up, texts and new words, language points explanation and practice, comprehensive exercises, and language tasks.

Learning objectives: Design the language functions, language points, medical knowledge, and social culture based on the text to help learners understand the learning focus of each lesson. With the improvement of learners' Chinese proficiency, this part uses Chinese.

Warm-up: Ask two questions to introduce the theme of the lesson, stimulate learners' interest in the content, and activate the background knowledge and related vocabulary they already acquired. The questions are on topics in daily communication and medicine.

Texts and new words: Each lesson includes three texts. Text 1 is a dialogue in medical scenarios, Text 2 is a dialogue in daily life, and Text 3 is a narration. In Volume 3, Text 3 discusses topics in daily life, and in Volume 4, it discusses medical topics. The correlation among the three texts and the recurrence of new words and grammar are emphasized. The new words are based on *Chinese Proficiency Test Syllabus* and *Medical Chinese Test (MCT) Syllabus*.

Language points explanation and practice: The language points are explained concisely and clearly using typical and abundant example sentences. Meanwhile, it highlights the summary of grammar points, the reminders of error-prone points, and the differentiation of synonyms. Each language point comes with targeted exercises.

Comprehensive exercises: After Text 1, Text 2 and Text 3, there are comprehensive exercises based on the texts and the development of knowledge and ability. The types of questions mainly include to "write Chinese characters according to Pinyin", "discriminate between Chinese characters and make words", "use the following words to fill in the blanks", "choose the correct positions of the following words in the sentences" "complete the dialogues with given words", "answer the following questions according to the text", and "fill in the blanks according to the text".

Language tasks: This part takes real-life situations as scenarios and guides students to complete comprehensive language tasks, such as "reading comprehension", "oral expression" and "written expression". Most language tasks are based on medical situations.

◎ Workbook

Each lesson consists of three parts: listening, reading and writing. The listening exercises include to "listen to sentences and judge right or wrong", and "listen to dialogues and choose the correct answers". The reading exercises include to "choose the correct context to fill in the blanks", "use the following words to fill in the blanks", "sort sentences", and "read the following paragraphs and choose the correct answers". The writing exercises include to "group the following words into sentences", "read the following sentences and write Chinese characters according to Pinyin", and "look at pictures and make sentences with given words".

5. Teaching Suggestions

We suggest that each lesson takes 6-8 class hours. If each week has 8 class hours, and each semester completes one volume if it has 16 weeks. If you choose the teaching mode of "main lecture + repetition drills", the "main lecture" teacher is responsible for teaching the texts, new words and language points, and guiding students to complete comprehensive exercises after the corresponding texts; the "repetition drills" teacher is responsible for teaching extended new words and language points, and helping students to complete the language tasks and the exercises in the workbook for each lesson.

6. Authoring Group

This series of textbooks are written by teachers with hands-on experience in medical Chinese. The compilers-in-chief are Zhu Ruilei and Zhen Zhen.

Textbook 1 and *Workbook 1* are written by Zhang Xingchun, Zhen Zhen, Zhang Juying, Li Xiaojing, and Zhu Ruilei. Zhang Xingchun is the finalizer.

Textbook 2 and *Workbook 2* are written by Zhang Juying, Zhang Xingchun, Li Xiaojing, Zhu Ruilei, Zhen Zhen, Zhang Haiping, and Li Tingyu. Zhang Juying is the finalizer.

Textbook 3 and *Workbook 3* are written by Zhen Zhen, Zhu Ruilei, Li Xiaojing, Zhang Juying, and Zhang Xingchun. Zhen Zhen is the finalizer.

Textbook 4 and *Workbook 4* are written by Li Xiaojing, Zhu Ruilei, Zhen Zhen, Zhang Juying and Zhang Xingchun. Li Xiaojing is the finalizer.

7. Accomplishments

This series of textbooks was tried out in Shandong University for three semesters by Zhang Xingchun, Zhu Ruilei, Dai Lihua, Zhou Wenfei, Xiao Xiao, Zhang Yun, Cai Yan, and other teachers. Zhang Haiping and Li Tingyu used it in Jiangxi University of Chinese Medicine for one semester before it is published. Ma Ling conducted a two-semester classroom trial at the University of Alabama. All of them have put forward many practical suggestions for the revision of the textbooks, and I would like to extend my special thanks.

When compiling these textbooks, Li An of Shandong University, provided strong technical support on word frequency statistics, and Chen Meng of Shandong University, conducted strict benchmarking with *Medical Chinese Test (MCT) Syllabus* in the selection of medical vocabulary, and Li Jingru, Xu Ziyu, Wen Lufei, Liu Xiaojie, Qi Zijun, Zhang Mingxin, Zeng Zheyu, and other students provided meticulous help in the organization of language data. Wang Xu, a doctor of Jinan Second People's Hospital, and Hou Yanmei, a doctor of Jinan Maternal and Child Health Hospital, provided their strong support in medical expertise and methods, and I would like to thank them all.

In addition, I would also like to thank Li Feifei, the editor in charge, of Beijing Language and Culture University Press, for her valuable comments on the revision of this series of textbooks.

The Authoring Group
April 2022

主要人物简介
Introductions to Major Characters

王 晨 / Wang Chen

中国人，男，19岁，东山大学基础医学院一年级学生。
Chinese, Male, 19 years old, Freshman of School of Basic Medical Science, Dongshan University.

李 真 / Li Zhen

中国人，女，18岁，东山大学文学院一年级学生。
Chinese, Female, 18 years old, Freshman of School of Literature, Dongshan University.

美 丽 / Meili

南非人，女，19岁，东山大学基础医学院一年级留学生。
South African, Female, 19 years old, International Freshman of School of Basic Medical Science, Dongshan University.

金 龙 / Jin Long

泰国人，男，21岁，东山大学基础医学院一年级留学生。
Thai, Male, 21 years old, International Freshman of School of Basic Medical Science, Dongshan University.

马大为 / Ma Dawei

尼泊尔人，男，20岁，东山大学基础医学院一年级留学生，金龙的同屋。
Nepalese, Male, 20 years old, International Freshman of School of Basic Medical Science, Dongshan University, Jin Long's roommate.

月 亮 / Yueliang

巴林人，女，20岁，东山大学基础医学院一年级留学生，美丽的同屋。
Bahraini, Female, 20 years old, International Freshman of School of Basic Medical Science, Dongshan University, Meili's roommate.

吉 米 / Jimmy

俄罗斯人，男，21岁，东山大学口腔医学院一年级留学生，马大为的朋友。
Russian, Male, 21 years old, International Freshman of School of Stomatology, Dongshan University, Ma Dawei's friend.

王 东 / Wang Dong

中国人，男，31岁，东山医院外科医生，王晨的哥哥。
Chinese, Male, 31 years old, Surgeon of Dongshan Hospital, Wang Chen's elder brother.

艺 文 / Yi Wen

中国人，女，32岁，东山医院眼科医生，王东的妻子。
Chinese, Female, 32 years old, Ophthalmologist of Dongshan Hospital, Wang Dong's wife.

张佳乐 / Zhang Jiale

中国人，女，28岁，东山医院护士，王东、艺文的朋友。
Chinese, Female, 28 years old, Nurse of Dongshan Hospital, Wang Dong and Yi Wen's friend.

刘一鸣 / Liu Yiming

中国人，男，30岁，律师，张佳乐的男朋友。
Chinese, Male, 30 years old, Lawyer, Zhang Jiale's boyfriend.

语法术语及缩略形式参照表
Grammar Terms and Their Abbreviations

Grammar Terms in Chinese	Grammar Terms in Pinyin	Grammar Terms in English	Abbreviations
名词	míngcí	noun	*n.*
代词	dàicí	pronoun	*pron.*
数词	shùcí	numeral	*num.*
量词	liàngcí	measure word	*m.*
数量词	shùliàngcí	numeral measure word	*num.-m.*
动词	dòngcí	verb	*v.*
能愿动词	néngyuàn dòngcí	modal verb	*mod.v.*
形容词	xíngróngcí	adjective	*adj.*
副词	fùcí	adverb	*adv.*
介词	jiècí	preposition	*prep.*
连词	liáncí	conjunction	*conj.*
助词	zhùcí	particle	*part.*
拟声词	nǐshēngcí	onomatopoeia	*onom.*
叹词	tàncí	interjection	*int.*
前缀	qiánzhuì	prefix	*pref.*
后缀	hòuzhuì	suffix	*suf.*
成语	chéngyǔ	idiom	*idm.*
主语	zhǔyǔ	subject	*S*
谓语	wèiyǔ	predicate	*P*
宾语	bīnyǔ	object	*O*
补语	bǔyǔ	complement	*C*
动宾结构	dòngbīn jiégòu	verb-object	*VO*
动补结构	dòngbǔ jiégòu	verb-complement	*VC*
动词性短语	dòngcíxìng duǎnyǔ	verbal phrase	*VP*
形容词性短语	xíngróngcíxìng duǎnyǔ	adjectival phrase	*AP*

目 录
Contents

汉语拼音（一）
Chinese Pinyin (1) ··· 1

拼音练习（一）
Pinyin exercises (1) ·· 5

汉语拼音（二）
Chinese Pinyin (2) ··· 7

拼音练习（二）
Pinyin exercises (2) ·· 8

汉语拼音（三）
Chinese Pinyin (3) ··· 10

拼音练习（三）
Pinyin exercises (3) ·· 13

第一课　你是学生吗？
　　　　Are you a student? ······································ 15

第二课　你叫什么名字？
　　　　What is your name? ····································· 26

第三课　你是哪国人？
　　　　Where are you from? ··································· 37

第四课　你有中国朋友吗？
　　　　Do you have Chinese friends? ························ 48

第五课 　我有五个外国朋友
　　　　　I have five foreign friends ················· 59

第六课 　今天几月几号？
　　　　　What's the date today? ··················· 71

第七课 　我们八点上课
　　　　　We start class at 8 o'clock ················· 85

第八课 　苹果多少钱一斤？
　　　　　How much is a *jin* of apples? ············· 102

第九课 　我哥哥在医院工作
　　　　　My elder brother works in a hospital ········· 117

第十课 　来我家玩儿吧！
　　　　　Come round to my home! ················· 131

第十一课 　解剖楼在图书馆的东边
　　　　　The anatomy building is to the east of the library ········· 145

第十二课 　菜做得太好吃了！
　　　　　The food is so delicious! ··················· 160

第十三课 　这儿不能抽烟
　　　　　No smoking here ······················· 175

第十四课 　这件白大褂是谁的？
　　　　　Whose white coat is this? ················· 188

第十五课 　天晴了
　　　　　The sky clears up ······················· 202

词汇总表
Glossary ·································· 216

汉语拼音（一）
Chinese Pinyin (1)

一、音节 Syllables

汉语里的音节一般包括三部分：声母、韵母和声调。例如 nǐ，n 是声母，i 是韵母，"ˇ"是声调。有的音节没有声母，只有韵母和声调。例如 è，e 是韵母，"ˋ"是声调。

A syllable in Chinese generally consists of three parts: the initial, the final, and the tone. For example: nǐ, n is the initial, i is the final, and "ˇ" is the tone. Some syllables have no initials, only finals and tones, such as è, e is the final, "ˋ" is the tone.

声母	+	韵母	+	声调	→	音节
initial	+	final	+	tone	→	syllable
n		i		ˇ	→	nǐ
h		ɑo		ˇ	→	hǎo
		e		ˋ	→	è

二、声母 Initials

声母位于音节的开头，汉语中一共有 21 个。按照发音部位和发音方法的不同，这 21 个声母可以分为以下六组：

The initials are located at the beginning of the syllables. There are 21 initials in Chinese. According to the pronunciation part and method, they are divided into the following six groups:

发音部位 Pronunciation part	发音方法 Pronunciation method						鼻音 Nasal	边音 Lateral sound
	塞音 Plosive		塞擦音 Affricate		擦音 Fricative			
	不送气 Unaspirated	送气 Aspirated	不送气 Unaspirated	送气 Aspirated	清 Voiceless	浊 Voiced		
双唇音 Bilabial	b	p					m	

1

（续表）

发音部位 Pronunciation part	发音方法　Pronunciation method							鼻音 Nasal	边音 Lateral sound
^^	塞音 Plosive		塞擦音 Affricate		擦音 Fricative		^^	^^
^^	不送气 Unaspirated	送气 Aspirated	不送气 Unaspirated	送气 Aspirated	清 Voiceless	浊 Voiced	^^	^^
唇齿音 Labiodental					f			
舌尖中音 Blade-alveolar	d	t					n	l
舌根音 Velar	g	k			h			
舌面音 Coronal			j	q	x			
舌尖后音 Blade-palatal			zh	ch	sh	r		
舌尖前音 Dental			z	c	s			

三、韵母 Finals

单韵母 (single vowel)：a　o　e　i　u　ü

四、声调 Tones

汉语中有四个声调，它们分别用符号"ˉ"（第一声）、"ˊ"（第二声）、"ˇ"（第三声）和"ˋ"（第四声）表示。

There are four tones in Chinese, which are represented by the symbols "ˉ" (the first tone), "ˊ" (the second tone), "ˇ" (the third tone), and "ˋ" (the fourth tone).

ā	á	ǎ	à
ō	ó	ǒ	ò
ē	é	ě	è
ī	í	ǐ	ì
ū	ú	ǔ	ù
ǖ	ǘ	ǚ	ǜ

mā	má	mǎ	mà
妈	麻	马	骂
mī	mí	mǐ	mì
眯	迷	米	秘

第一声，55调；第二声，35调；第三声，214调；第四声，51调。具体如下图所示：
The first tone is in the pitch of 55; the second tone is in the pitch of 35; the third tone is in the pitch of 214; the fourth tone is in the pitch of 51. As shown below:

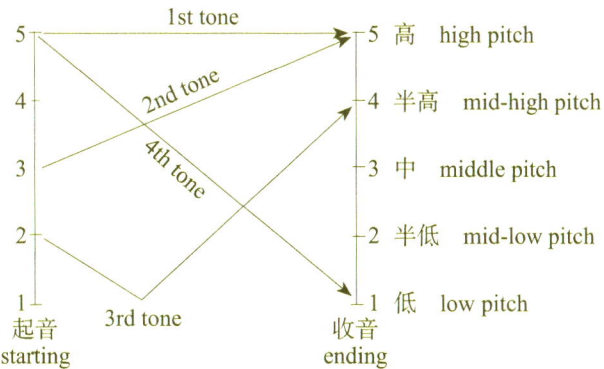

五、声韵拼合 The combination of initials and finals

声母 Initials	韵母 Finals					
	a	o	e	i	u	ü
b	ba	bo		bi	bu	
p	pa	po		pi	pu	
m	ma	mo	me	mi	mu	
f	fa	fo			fu	
d	da		de	di	du	
t	ta		te	ti	tu	
n	na		ne	ni	nu	nü
l	la		le	li	lu	lü
g	ga		ge		gu	
k	ka		ke		ku	
h	ha		he		hu	
j				ji		ju
q				qi		qu
x				xi		xu
z	za		ze		zu	
c	ca		ce		cu	
s	sa		se		su	
zh	zha		zhe		zhu	
ch	cha		che		chu	

（续表）

声母 Initials	韵母 Finals					
	a	o	e	i	u	ü
sh	sha		she		shu	
r			re		ru	

拼音练习（一）
Pinyin exercises (1)

一、朗读下面的音节 Read aloud the following syllables

1. bā   bá   bǎ   bà
2. mō   mó   mǒ   mò
3. fū   fú   fǔ   fù
4. dī   dí   dǐ   dì
5. kē   ké   kě   kè
6. lū   lú   lǔ   lù
7. qī   qí   qǐ   qì
8. xū   xú   xǔ   xù

二、听录音，选出你听到的音节 Listen to the recording and pick out the syllables you hear

1. bù——pù   8. fú——hú
2. dǎ——tǎ   9. gē——kē
3. jì——zì   10. qǐ——xǐ
4. nǔ——lǔ   11. zhǐ——chǐ
5. mā——mǎ   12. dú——dù
6. sā——sǎ   13. lí——lì
7. zhé——zhè   14. sǐ——sì

三、朗读下面的词语 Read aloud the following words

1. bà

2. mā

3. mǐ

4. hē

5. jī

6. zì

7. shū

8. rè

日常用语 Daily talk

1. 你好!	Nǐ hǎo!	Hello!
2. 谢谢!	Xièxie!	Thanks!
3. 不客气。	Bú kèqi.	You are welcome.
4. 对不起。	Duìbuqǐ.	Sorry.
5. 没关系。	Méi guānxi.	It doesn't matter.
6. 再见!	Zàijiàn!	Bye!

汉语拼音（二）
Chinese Pinyin (2)

一、复韵母 Complex vowels

ai	ei	ao	ou	
ia	ie	ua	uo	üe
iao	iou	uai	uei	

二、鼻韵母 Nasal vowels

an	ian	uan	üan
en	in	uen	ün
ang	iang	uang	
eng	ing	ueng	
		ong	iong

三、卷舌元音 er Retroflex vowel "er"

卷舌元音 er 可以单独构成音节，例如：ér（儿）、ěr（耳）、èr（二）。

The retroflex vowel er can form syllables alone, such as ér (儿, child), ěr (耳, ear), and èr (二, two).

卷舌元音 er 常与其他韵母结合在一起，成为儿化韵母，其书写形式是在原韵母后加 r。例如：huàr（画儿）、xiǎohái r（小孩儿）、yíhuìr（一会儿）。

The retroflex vowel er is often combined with other finals to form an r-ending final. In transcription it is shown by adding an r to the original final, for example huàr (画儿, painting), xiǎohái r (小孩儿, children), and yíhuìr (一会儿, for a while).

拼音练习（二）
Pinyin exercises (2)

一、朗读下面的音节 Read aloud the following syllables

1. bāi	bái	bǎi	bài
2. xiān	xián	xiǎn	xiàn
3. guāi		guǎi	guài
4. jīng		jǐng	jìng
5. tāi	tái	tǎi	tài
6. zhēn		zhěn	zhèn

二、听录音，选出你听到的音节 Listen to the recording and pick out the syllables you hear

1. bái——běi
2. jìn——jìng
3. jiào——xiǎo
4. ér——ěr
5. xiě——xiè
6. kuā——kuà

7. bēn——pēn
8. qǐng——xǐng
9. quē——xué
10. ěr——èr
11. gǒu——gòu
12. huār——huàr

三、朗读下面的词语 Read aloud the following words

1. lǎoshī

2. xuéshēng

3. kàn shū

4. jiàoshì

5. chīfàn

6. shítáng

7. gāoxìng

8. yuèliang

日常用语 Daily talk

1. 上课。	Shàngkè.	Class is begin.
2. 下课。	Xiàkè.	Class is over.
3. 打开书。	Dǎkāi shū.	Open your book.
4. 跟我读。	Gēn wǒ dú.	Read after me.
5. 读生词。	Dú shēngcí.	Read the new words.
6. 写汉字。	Xiě Hànzì.	Write the characters.

汉语拼音（三）
Chinese Pinyin (3)

一、轻声 The neutral tone

除了四个声调以外，汉语里有的音节读轻声。轻声发音短而轻，在书写时不加调号。例如：

Besides the four tones, there are some toneless syllables in Chinese, which are pronounced relatively short and light. In transcription a neutral tone does not carry any tone mark. For example:

bàba	dìdi	jiějie	māma
爸爸	弟弟	姐姐	妈妈
bēizi	péngyou	xiūxi	rènshi
杯子	朋友	休息	认识
wǒmen	nǐmen	tāmen	zánmen
我们	你们	他们	咱们
duìbuqǐ	méi guānxi	bú kèqi	
对不起	没关系	不客气	

二、三声变调 The third tone sandhi

1. 三声 + 三声 The third tone + the third tone

当两个三声的音节连在一起时，第一个音节变成第二声，第二个音节声调不变。例如："nǐ hǎo（你好）"的发音变成"ní hǎo（你好）"。

When two third-tone syllables show in succession, the former is pronounced as the second tone as the latter remains unchanged. For example, "nǐ hǎo（你好）" is pronounced as "ní hǎo（你好）".

2. 三声 + 非三声 The third tone + the non-third tone

当三声后跟一声、二声、四声以及大部分轻声时，三声要变成"半三声"，就是只读三声前面一半的声调。例如"nǐ jiā（你家）""nǐ lái（你来）""nǐ qù（你去）"和"nǐmen（你们）"中的"nǐ（你）"都要读成"半三声"。

When a third-tone syllable shows with a first-tone, second-tone, forth-tone syllable or one of the most light-tone syllables in succession, it changes into a "half third tone", which means only the first half of the tone is articulated, such as the "nǐ（你）" in "nǐ jiā（你家）" "nǐ lái（你来）" "nǐ qù（你去）" and "nǐmen（你们）".

三、拼写规则 Spelling rules

（1）i、u、ü 自成音节时，要写成 yi、wu、yu。

When the finals i, u, and ü stand alone as a syllable, they should be written as yi, wu, and yu.

（2）ia、ie、iao、iou、ian、iang、iong 自成音节时，要写成 ya、ye、yao、you、yan、yang、yong。

When the finals ia, ie, iao, iou, ian, iang, and iong stand alone as a syllable, they should be written as ya, ye, yao, you, yan, yang, and yong.

in、ing 自成音节时，要写成 yin、ying。

When the finals in and ing stand alone as a syllable, they should be written as yin and ying.

（3）ua、uo、uai、uei、uan、uen、uang、ueng 自成音节时，写成 wa、wo、wai、wei、wan、wen、wang、weng。

When the finals ua, uo, uai, uei, uan, uen, uang, and ueng stand alone as a syllable, they are written as wa, wo, wai, wei, wan, wen, wang, and weng.

（4）üe、üan、ün 自成音节时，要写成 yue、yuan、yun。

When the finals üe, üan, and ün stand alone as a syllable, they should be written as yue, yuan, and yun.

ü、üe、üan、ün 位于声母 j、q、x 后边时，头上的两点要省略，写成 u。例如："jù（句）""xué（学）""quán（全）""jūn（军）"。

When ü, üe, üan, and ün are located after the initials j, q, and x, the two dots above should be omitted and written as u. For example: "jù (句, sentence)" "xué (学, to learn)" "quán (全, all)" "jūn (军, army)".

（5）复韵母 iou 与声母相拼合时，写成 iu，声调标在 u 上。例如："jiǔ（九）""liù（六）"。

When the complex vowel iou is put together with initials, it should be written as iu while the tone is marked on u, such as "jiǔ(九, nine)" and "liù(六, six)".

（6）复韵母 uei、uen 与声母相拼合时，分别写成 ui、un，声调分别标在 i、u 上。

汉语拼音（三）
Chinese Pinyin (3)

例如："guì（贵）" "kùn（困）"。

When the complex vowel uei and uen is put together with initials, they should be written as ui and un while the tones are marked on i and u, such as "guì (贵, expensive)" and "kùn (困, tired)".

（7）当 a、o、e 开头的音节出现在别的音节之后时，如果音节的界限发生混淆，那要用隔音符号" ' "隔开。例如："Xī'ān（西安）" "nǚ'ér（女儿）"。

When a syllable starting with a, o and e shows after other syllables, once the boundaries of syllables are confused, they need to be separated by separation mark " ' ", such as "Xī'ān (西安, Xi'an)" and "nǚ'ér (女儿, daughter)".

拼音练习（三）
Pinyin exercises (3)

一、朗读下面的词语 Read aloud the following words

1. 轻声 The neutral tone

1. bàba	māma	nǎinai	gēge
2. dìdi	wǒmen	nǐmen	xièxie
3. bēizi	háizi	péngyou	duìbuqǐ

2. 三声变调 The third tone sandhi

1. nǐ hǎo	hěn hǎo	shǒubiǎo	xǐzǎo
2. gǔdiǎn	xiǎojiě	yǒnggǎn	zǎodiǎn
3. lǎoshī	yǒu qián	hǎokàn	nǐmen

二、请按照正确的拼写规则改写下面的音节 Please rewrite the following syllables according to the spelling rules

í_____	ǔ_____	jiōu_____
uǒ_____	ùe_____	guěn_____
iān_____	jǜ_____	Xīan_____
uáng_____	xüān_____	duèi_____

日常用语 Daily talk

1. 老师	lǎoshī	teacher
2. 作业	zuòyè	homework
3. 听写	tīngxiě	dictation
4. 看黑板。	Kàn hēibǎn.	Look at the blackboard.
5. 听不懂。	Tīng bù dǒng.	I don't understand.
6. 再说一遍。	Zài shuō yí biàn.	Repeat.

第一课 Lesson 1

Nǐ shì xuéshēng ma?
你是 学生 吗?
Are you a student?

学习目标 Learning Objectives

1. Language Function: Greet each other.
2. Language Points: "是"–sentence; Modal particle "吗" and non–interrogative sentence; Adverb "不".

热身活动 Warming-up

1. 你知道怎么用汉语互相问候吗?
   Do you know how to greet each other in Chinese?

2. 你知道在汉语里"老师"怎么说吗?
   Do you know how to say "teacher" in Chinese?

课文（一）
Text（Ⅰ）

(Wang Chen meets Meili for the first time on campus.)

Wáng Chén: Nǐ hǎo!
王晨： 你 好！

Měilì: Nǐ hǎo!
美丽： 你 好！

Wáng Chén: Nǐ shì xuéshēng ma?
王晨： 你 是 学生 吗？

Měilì: Wǒ shì xuéshēng.
美丽： 我 是 学生。

Wáng Chén: Nǐ shì liúxuéshēng ma?
王晨： 你 是 留学生 吗？

Měilì: Wǒ shì liúxuéshēng.
美丽： 我 是 留学生。

Wang Chen: Hello!
    Meili: Hello!
Wang Chen: Are you a student?
    Meili: Yes, I am.
Wang Chen: Are you an international student?
    Meili: Yes, I am.

生词 New words

1. 你	nǐ	*pron.*	you
2. 好	hǎo	*adj.*	good, well, fine
3. 是	shì	*v.*	to be, is/am/are
4. 学生	xuéshēng	*n.*	student
5. 吗	ma	*part.*	used at the end of a sentence to indicate a question
6. 我	wǒ	*pron.*	I, me
7. 留学生	liúxuéshēng	*n.*	international student

留学　　　　　liúxué　　　v.　　　　to study abroad

专名 Proper nouns

1. 王晨　　　　Wáng Chén　　　　name of a Chinese student
2. 美丽　　　　Měilì　　　　　　name of a South African student

语言点 Language Points

一、"是"字句　"是"-sentence

"是"字句是由动词"是"连接前后两个部分的句子，表示肯定或判断。例如：

The verb "是" connects the front and back parts of a "是" sentence, which expresses a definite or judgmental attitude.

1. 我是学生。
2. 我是留学生。
3. 我是王晨。

※ 练习：组词成句 Group words into sentences

1. 学生　是　我

   _____。

2. 是　留学生　我

   _____。

3. 美丽　是　我

   _____。

二、语气助词"吗"和是非疑问句
Modal particle "吗" and non-interrogative sentence

语气助词"吗"表示疑问，可用在陈述句句尾，构成疑问句。这种疑问句叫是非疑问句，要求对方做出肯定或否定的回答。

The modal particle "吗", put at the end of a narrative sentence, expresses an interrogative attitude. It forms a non-interrogative sentence, that is, a yes or no question.

做肯定回答时，说话人去掉问句中的"吗"就可以。例如：

As for a positive answer of such questions, the speaker just needs to remove "吗" of the question. For example:

1. A：你是学生吗？
   B：我是学生。
2. A：你是留学生吗？
   B：我是留学生。

做否定回答时，说话人要在动词或形容词前边加上否定副词"不（bù, not）"。例如：

And as for a negative answer, the speaker should add the negative adverb "不 (bù, not)" in front of a verb or an adjective. For example:

3. A：你是王晨吗？
   B：我不是王晨。

※ 练习：请用带"吗"的是非疑问句提问

　　　　Please make non-interrogative sentences with "吗"

1. A：_____？
   B：我是留学生。
2. A：_____？
   B：我是学生。
3. A：_____？
   B：我是美丽。

综合练习 Comprehensive Exercises

一、听录音，选出你听到的音节 Listen to the recording and pick out the syllables you hear

1. A. nǐ   B. lǐ
2. A. wǎng   B. wǒ
3. A. liú   B. niú

4. A. shì   B. sì
5. A. xié   B. xué
6. A. hǎo   B. xiǎo

二、根据汉字写拼音 Write Pinyin according to Chinese characters

1. 学生_____
2. 吗_____
3. 是_____
4. 好_____
5. 我_____
6. 你_____

三、朗读语句 Read aloud

1. 你好
2. 学生
3. 留学生

4. 你是学生吗？
5. 我是学生。
6. 我是留学生。

四、完成对话 Complete dialogues

王晨：你好！你是_____？

美丽：我是学生。

王晨：_____留学生吗？

美丽：我是留学生。

五、汉字书写 Write Chinese characters

你	亻+尔										
	ノ	亻	亻	你	你	你	你				
好	女+子										
	く	乂	女	如	好	好					
学	兴+子										
	丶	丷	丷	丷	兴	学	学	学			
生	ノ	ト	仁	牛	生						
吗	口+马										
	丨	口	口	吗	吗	吗					
是	日+疋										
	丨	口	日	日	旦	早	早	昰	是		

课文（二）
Text (Ⅱ)

(Jin Long meets Mr Wang at the gate of the teaching building.)

Jīn Lóng: Nǐ hǎo!
金龙：你好！

Wáng lǎoshī: Nǐ hǎo!
王老师：你好！

Jīn Lóng: Nǐ shì xuéshēng ma?
金龙：你是学生吗？

Wáng lǎoshī: Wǒ bú shì xuéshēng, wǒ shì lǎoshī.
王老师：我不是学生，我是老师。

Jīn Lóng: Duìbuqǐ.
金龙：对不起。

Wáng lǎoshī: Méi guānxi.
王老师：没关系。

Jīn Lóng: Lǎoshī, zàijiàn.
金龙：老师，再见。

Wáng lǎoshī: Zàijiàn.
王老师：再见。

Jin Long: Hello!
Mr Wang: Hello!
Jin Long: Are you a student?
Mr Wang: No, I am not a student. I am a teacher.
Jin Long: Sorry.
Mr Wang: It's OK.
Jin Long: See you, sir.
Mr Wang: See you.

第一课 你是学生吗？
Lesson 1 Are you a student?

生词 New words

1. 不　　　　　bù　　　　　*adv.*　　　no, not
2. 老师　　　　lǎoshī　　　*n.*　　　　teacher
3. 对不起　　　duìbuqǐ　　 *v.*　　　　I'm sorry; excuse me
4. 没关系　　　méi guānxi　*VO*　　　 it doesn't matter; it's OK
5. 再见　　　　zàijiàn　　　*v.*　　　　see you; goodbye

专名 Proper nouns

1. 金龙　　　　Jīn Lóng　　　　　name of a Thai student
2. 王　　　　　Wáng　　　　　　a surname in Chinese

语言点 Language Points

副词"不"　Adverb "不"

副词"不"表示否定，一般用在动词或形容词的前边。例如：

The adverb "不" means denial and is usually used before a verb or an adjective. For example:

1. 我不是学生。
2. 我不是留学生。
3. 我不是老师。
4. 我不好。

注意："不"在四声字前读二声，例如"bú shì（不是）""bú jiàn（不见）"；在一声、二声、三声字前不变调，还读四声，例如"bù gāo（不高）""bù xíng（不行）""bù hǎo（不好）"。

Attention: "不" is pronounced as the second tone before a forth tone syllable, such as "bú shì（不是）" and "bú jiàn（不见）". When it shows before a first-tone, second-tone or third-tone, it is pronounced as the forth tone, such as "bù gāo（不高）" "bù xíng（不行）" and "bù hǎo（不好）".

※ 练习：请用否定句回答问题
　　　　Please answer the questions with negative sentences

1. A：你是学生吗？
   B：_____。

2. A：你是老师吗？
   B：_____。

3. A：你是留学生吗？
   B：_____。

4. A：你好吗？
   B：_____。

综合练习 Comprehensive Exercises

一、听录音，选出你听到的音节 Listen to the recording and pick out the syllables you hear

1. A. bú   B. bù
2. A. lǎo   B. nǎo
3. A. shēng   B. shēn

4. A. qǐ   B. jǐ
5. A. duì   B. tuì
6. A. jiàn   B. qiàn

二、根据汉字写拼音 Write Pinyin according to Chinese characters

1. 不_____
2. 再见_____
3. 对不起_____
4. 王_____
5. 老师_____
6. 没关系_____

第一课　你是学生吗？
Lesson 1　Are you a student?

三、朗读语句 Read aloud

1. 对不起
2. 没关系
3. 再见

4. 老师好!
5. 老师,对不起!
6. 老师,再见!

四、完成对话 Complete dialogues

王老师:你好!

金　龙:你好!你是学生吗?

王老师:我_____,我是老师。

金　龙:对不起。

王老师:_____。

金　龙:_____,再见。

王老师:再见。

五、汉字书写 Write Chinese characters

不	一	丆	不	不							
我	ノ	一	于	手	我	我	我				
关	丶	丷	业	兰	关	关					
再	一	厂	冂	币	冉	再					
见	丨	冂	贝	见							
对	又+寸										
	乛	又	对	对	对						

语言任务 Language Tasks

一、阅读理解 Reading comprehension

王晨、美丽是学生，美丽是留学生。我不是学生，是老师。

读后判断 True or false

1. "我"是学生。　　　　　　　　　　　　　　　　　（　）
2. 王晨是留学生。　　　　　　　　　　　　　　　　（　）
3. 美丽是学生。　　　　　　　　　　　　　　　　　（　）

二、口头表达 Oral expression

任务名称：问候。

Task: Greet each other.

任务要求：两名学生一组，互相打招呼。

Requirements: Work in pairs and greet each other.

Reference words: 是　吗　学生　老师　不　对不起　没关系　再见

第二课 Lesson 2

Nǐ jiào shénme míngzi?
你叫 什么 名字?
What is your name?

学习目标 Learning Objectives

1. Language Function: Ask someone's name or introduce your own name.
2. Language Points: Interrogative pronoun "什么"; Adjective predicate sentence; Adverb "也"; Modal particle "呢" (1).

热身活动 Warming-up

1. 你的中文名字叫什么?
What's your Chinese name?

2. 你知道初次见面时中国人会说什么吗?
Do you know what the Chinese say when they first meet?

课文（一）
Text (I)

(Ma Dawei meets Li Zhen for the first time on campus.)

Mǎ Dàwéi: Nǐ hǎo!
马大为：你好！

Lǐ Zhēn: Nǐ hǎo!
李真：你好！

Mǎ Dàwéi: Nǐ jiào shénme míngzi?
马大为：你叫什么名字？

Lǐ Zhēn: Wǒ jiào Lǐ Zhēn. Nǐ jiào shénme míngzi?
李真：我叫李真。你叫什么名字？

Mǎ Dàwéi: Wǒ jiào Mǎ Dàwéi, rènshi nǐ hěn gāoxìng.
马大为：我叫马大为，认识你很高兴。

Lǐ Zhēn: Rènshi nǐ, wǒ yě hěn gāoxìng.
李真：认识你，我也很高兴。

Ma Dawei: Hello!
Li Zhen: Hello!
Ma Dawei: What's your name?
Li Zhen: My name is Li Zhen. What's your name?
Ma Dawei: My name is Ma Dawei. Nice to meet you.
Li Zhen: Nice to meet you, too.

生词 New words

1. 叫	jiào	v.	to be called
2. 什么	shénme	pron.	what
3. 名字	míngzi	n.	name
4. 认识	rènshi	v.	to know
5. 很	hěn	adv.	very
6. 高兴	gāoxìng	adj.	happy, glad
7. 也	yě	adv.	too, also

第二课　你叫什么名字？
Lesson 2　What is your name?

专名 Proper nouns

1. 马大为　　　　Mǎ Dàwéi　　　　name of a Nepalese student
2. 李真　　　　　Lǐ Zhēn　　　　　name of a Chinese student

语言点 Language Points

一、疑问代词"什么"　Interrogative pronoun "什么"

疑问代词"什么"可以用来询问人、事物、时间、地点等。有疑问代词的问句的语序与陈述句相同。例如：

The interrogative pronoun "什么" can be used to ask about people, things and matters, time, place and so on. The order of the question with an interrogative pronoun is the same as the narrative sentence. For example:

1. 你叫什么名字？
2. 你叫什么？
3. 老师叫什么名字？

※ 练习：回答问题　Answer the questions

1. 你叫什么名字？
　　_____。

2. 老师叫什么名字？
　　_____。

二、形容词谓语句　Adjective predicate sentence

在汉语里，形容词可以直接充当谓语，前面常有"很"等程度副词。形容词谓语句的基本结构是"主语＋程度副词＋形容词"，其否定形式是"主语＋不＋形容词"，疑问形式是"主语＋形容词＋吗？"。例如：

In Chinese, adjectives can act as predicates directly, often preceded by degree adverbs such as "很". The basic structure of an adjective predicate sentence is "subject + degree adverb + adjective". The negative structure is "subject + 不 + adjective". The interrogative structure is "subject + adjective + 吗？". For example:

1. 我很高兴。

2. 美丽不高兴。

3. 你高兴吗？

※ 练习：完成对话 Complete dialogues

1. A：老师好吗？
   B：_____。

2. A：你高兴吗？
   B：_____。

3. A：_____？
   B：马大为不高兴。

三、副词"也"　Adverb "也"

副词"也"表示情况相同，常用在主语之后，动词或形容词之前。如果用在否定句中，副词"也"应置于"不"的前边。例如：

The adverb "也" means the same. It is put between the subject and the verb or the adjective. In a negative sentence, "也" should be put in front of "不". For example:

1. 美丽是留学生，马大为也是留学生。

2. 你很高兴，我也很高兴。

3. 马大为不高兴，美丽也不高兴。

※ 练习：组词成句 Group words into sentences

1. 好　很　也　老师

_____。

2. 高兴　美丽　也　不

　　_____。

3. 学生　是　也　王晨

　　_____。

综合练习 Comprehensive Exercises

一、听录音，选出你听到的音节 Listen to the recording and pick out the syllables you hear

1. A. míng　　B. píng
2. A. jiào　　B. xiào
3. A. rěn　　B. hěn

4. A. zhēn　　B. chēn
5. A. shén　　B. shéng
6. A. yě　　B. xiě

二、根据汉字写拼音 Write Pinyin according to Chinese characters

1. 很_____
2. 什么_____
3. 高兴_____
4. 也_____
5. 认识_____
6. 名字_____

三、朗读语句 Read aloud

1. 我不认识你。
2. 你叫什么？
3. 我很高兴。

4. 认识你很高兴。
5. 我也很高兴。
6. 老师叫什么名字？

四、完成对话 Complete dialogues

马大为：你好！

李　真：你好！

马大为：你_____？

李　真：我叫李真。你叫什么名字？

马大为：我叫马大为，_____。

李　真：认识你，我_____很高兴。

五、汉字书写 Write Chinese characters

叫	口 + 丩
	丨 口 口 叫 叫
什	亻 + 十
	丿 亻 仁 什
么	丿 么 么
名	夕 + 口
	丿 ク 夕 夕 名 名
字	宀 + 子
	丶 丷 宀 宀 宁 字
很	彳 + 艮
	丿 彳 彳 彳 彳 彳 彳 很 很

课文（二）
Text (II)

(The teacher and the students get to know each other on the first day of a new semester.)

Mǎ Dàwéi: Lǎoshī, qǐngwèn nín guìxìng?
马大为：老师，请问 您贵姓？

Wáng lǎoshī: Wǒ xìng Wáng.
王老师：我 姓 王。

Mǎ Dàwéi, Wáng Chén: Wáng lǎoshī, nín hǎo!
马大为、王晨：王 老师，您好！

Wáng lǎoshī: Nǐmen hǎo! Nǐmen jiào shénme míngzi?
王老师：你们 好！你们 叫 什么 名字？

Wáng Chén: Wǒ yě xìng Wáng, jiào Wáng Chén.
王晨：我 也姓 王，叫 王 晨。

Wáng lǎoshī: Nǐ ne?
王老师：你呢？

Mǎ Dàwéi: Wǒ jiào Mǎ Dàwéi.
马大为：我 叫马大为。

Ma Dawei: Sir, may I have your family name?
Mr Wang: My family name is Wang.
Ma Dawei, Wang Chen: Hello, Mr Wang!
Mr Wang: Mr Wang:Hello! What's your names?
Wang Chen: My family name is also Wang, and my name is Wang Chen.
Mr Wang: Mr Wang:What about you?
Ma Dawei: My name is Ma Dawei.

生词 New words

1. 请问	qǐngwèn	v.	excuse me, please
请	qǐng	v.	please
问	wèn	v.	to ask
2. 您	nín	pron.	you, respectful form of 你
3. 贵姓	guìxìng	n.	(your honorable) surname
贵	guì		your (used to modify things of the other part of the conversation to show respect)
姓	xìng	n./v.	family name, surname; one's surname is
4. 你们	nǐmen	pron.	you (plural)
们	men	suf.	used after a personal pronoun or a noun to show plural number
5. 呢	ne	part.	marker of a special, alternative or rhetorical question

语言点 Language Points

语气助词"呢"（1） Modal particle "呢" (1)

语气助词"呢"可以用在名词、名词性短语或代词后构成疑问句。这种用法一般出现在问题已经明确的语境中，用来承接上文提出的问题。例如：

The modal particle "呢" is put after a noun, nominal phrase or pronoun to make an interrogative sentence. It is usually used in the context that the question is clear to carry on the question raised above. For example:

1. A：王晨是留学生吗？
   B：王晨不是留学生。
   A：马大为呢？
   B：马大为是留学生。

2. A：你是学生吗？
   B：我是学生。你呢？

第二课 你叫什么名字？
Lesson 2 What is your name?

A：我也是学生。

3. A：你高兴吗?

B：我很高兴。你呢?

A：我也很高兴。

※ 练习：回答问题 Answer the questions

1. 我是老师。你呢?
   _____。

2. 我姓王。你呢?
   _____。

3. 认识王晨我很高兴。你呢?
   _____。

综合练习 Comprehensive Exercises

一、听录音，选出你听到的音节 Listen to the recording and pick out the syllables you hear

1. A. xìng   B. xìn
2. A. qǐng   B. xǐng
3. A. guì   B. huì

4. A. ne   B. le
5. A. wèn   B. wēng
6. A. wáng   B. wán

二、根据汉字写拼音 Write Pinyin according to Chinese characters

1. 贵_____   3. 请问_____   5. 姓_____

2. 呢_____   4. 您_____   6. 你们_____

三、朗读语句 Read aloud

1. 请问
2. 贵姓
3. 您好
4. 请问您贵姓？
5. 我姓王。
6. 我也姓王。

四、完成对话 Complete dialogues

马大为：老师，请问您_____？

王老师：我姓王。

马大为、王晨：王老师，您好！

王老师：你们好！你们_____名字？

王　晨：我也_____王，叫王晨。

王老师：你呢？

马大为：我_____马大为。

五、汉字书写 Write Chinese characters

请	讠+青
	丶 讠 讠 诂 诉 诘 请 请 请
问	门+口
	丶 门 门 问 问
您	你+心
	丿 亻 亻 伱 你 你 你 您 您 您
贵	虫+贝
	丶 口 口 虫 虫 虫 贵 贵
姓	女+生
	ㄑ 女 女 女 妁 姓 姓

第二课　你叫什么名字？
Lesson 2　What is your name?

们	亻+门										
	丿	亻	亻	伊	们						

语言任务 Language Tasks

一、阅读理解 Reading comprehension

　　我姓王，叫王晨。我是学生。她（tā，she）的名字叫李真，她姓李，也是学生。认识她，我很高兴。

读后判断 True or false

1. "我"姓王晨。　　　　　　　　　　　　　　　　　　　（　）

2. 王晨是留学生。　　　　　　　　　　　　　　　　　　（　）

3. 李真也是学生。　　　　　　　　　　　　　　　　　　（　）

4. 认识李真，王晨很高兴。　　　　　　　　　　　　　　（　）

二、口头表达 Oral expression

任务名称：询问姓名。

Task: Ask for names.

任务要求：两名学生一组，互相询问姓名。

Requirements: Work in pairs and ask each other's name.

Reference words: 认识　很　高兴　请问　贵姓　也　呢

第三课 Lesson 3

Nǐ shì nǎ guó rén?
你是哪国人?
Where are you from?

学习目标 Learning Objectives

1. Language Function: Ask about someone's nationality and introduce your own nation.
2. Language Points: Interrogative pronoun "哪"; Yes-no question; Adverb "都" (1); Structural particle "的"; Interrogative pronoun "谁".

热身活动 Warming-up

1. 你是哪国人?
   Where are you from?

2. 你知道你的同学是哪国人吗?
   Do you know where are your classmates from?

课文（一）
Text (Ⅰ)

(Meili meets Jin Long and his friend.)

Jīn Lóng: Nǐ shì nǎ guó rén?
金龙：你是哪国人？

Měilì: Wǒ shì Nánfēirén, nǐ ne?
美丽：我是南非人，你呢？

Jīn Lóng: Wǒ shì Tàiguórén.
金龙：我是泰国人。

Měilì: Tā yě shì Tàiguórén, duì ma?
美丽：他也是泰国人，对吗？

Jīn Lóng: Duì, tā yě shì. Wǒmen dōu shì Tàiguó liúxuéshēng.
金龙：对，他也是。我们都是泰国留学生。

Jin Long: Where are you from?
　　Meili: I'm a South African, and you?
Jin Long: I'm a Thai.
　　Meili: Is he a Thai, too?
Jin Long: Yes, he is. We're both Thai students.

生词 New words

1. 哪	nǎ	*pron.*	which
2. 国	guó	*n.*	country
3. 人	rén	*n.*	person
4. 他	tā	*pron.*	he, him
5. 对	duì	*adj.*	right
6. 我们	wǒmen	*pron.*	we, us
7. 都	dōu	*adv.*	both, all

专名 Proper nouns

1. 南非	Nánfēi	South Africa
2. 泰国	Tàiguó	Thailand

语言点 Language Points

一、疑问代词"哪"　Interrogative pronoun "哪"

疑问代词"哪"常用来询问人或事物。例如：

The interrogative pronoun "哪" is often used to ask about people or things. For example:

1. 你是哪国人？
2. 王老师是哪国人？
3. 美丽是哪国留学生？

※ 练习：回答问题　Answer the questions

1. 美丽是哪国人？

　　_____。

2. 金龙是哪国留学生？

　　_____。

3. 王晨是哪国学生？

　　_____。

二、是非疑问句　Yes-no question

在是非疑问句中，说话人提出自己的想法或建议后，询问对方的意见，对方应给出肯定或否定的答复。例如：

In yes-no questions, after the speaker has offered his or her own idea or suggestion and asks the other person for his or her opinion, a "yes" or "no" answer is generally required. For example:

1. 他也是泰国人，对吗？
2. 美丽是留学生，对吗？
3. 老师很高兴，对吗？

※ 练习：完成对话 Complete dialogues

1. A：你是留学生，对吗？

   B：_____。

2. A：你不高兴，对吗？

   B：_____。

3. A：_____？

   B：对，他也姓李。

三、副词"都"（1） Adverb "都" (1)

副词"都"表示范围，常用在主语后面、动词或形容词前面，总括前面的人或事物。例如：

The adverb "都" indicates range and is often used between the subject and the verb or adjective to sum up the people or things raised above. For example:

1. 我们都是留学生。

2. 王晨、美丽、马大为都是学生。

3. 我们都很高兴。

在否定句中，"都"用在"不"的前面和后面时，句子意思不同。例如：

In a negative sentence, "都" put before or after "不" would make different meanings. For example:

4. 王晨不是老师，金龙也不是老师，他们（tāmen, they）都不是老师。

5. 我是老师，他不是老师，我们不都是老师。

※ 练习：回答问题 Answer the questions

1. 你们都是学生吗？

   _____。

2. 王晨和李真都是留学生吗？

   _____。

3. 美丽和金龙都是南非人吗？

   _____。

综合练习 Comprehensive Exercises

一、听录音，选出你听到的音节 Listen to the recording and pick out the syllables you hear

1. A. zhū　　B. jū
2. A. nǎ　　B. là
3. A. guó　　B. kuò
4. A. rán　　B. rén
5. A. dōu　　B. tōu
6. A. rén　　B. rèn

二、根据汉字写拼音 Write Pinyin according to Chinese characters

1. 哪_____　　3. 对_____　　5. 都_____

2. 国_____　　4. 他_____　　6. 人_____

三、朗读语句 Read aloud

1. 很高兴
2. 都认识
3. 哪国人
4. 你是哪国人？
5. 我是中国人（Zhōngguórén, Chinese）。
6. 他是南非人。

四、完成对话 Complete dialogues

金龙：你是哪国人？

美丽：我是_____，你_____？

金龙：我是泰国人。

美丽：他_____是泰国人，_____吗？

金龙：对，他也是。我们_____是泰国留学生。

第三课　你是哪国人？
Lesson 3　Where are you from?

五、汉字书写 Write Chinese characters

哪	口 + 那												
	丨	口	口	叮	叼	吗	呗	哪	哪				
国	口 + 玉												
	丨	冂	冂	月	用	国	国	国					
人	丿	人											
南	十 + 冂												
	一	十	广	冇	冇	南	南	南					
都	者 + 阝												
	一	十	土	耂	耂	者	者	者	者	都			
他	亻 + 也												
	丿	亻	仢	他	他								

课文（二）
Text (Ⅱ)

(Ma Dawei is reading in the dormitory.)

Jīn Lóng: Zhè shì nǐ de shū ma?
金龙：这是你的书吗？

Mǎ Dàwéi: Bú shì, zhè shì Lǐ Zhēn de shū. Nàxiē shì wǒ de shū.
马大为：不是，这是李真的书。那些是我的书。

Jīn Lóng: Lǐ Zhēn shì shéi?
金龙：李真是谁？

Mǎ Dàwéi: Tā shì wǒ de péngyou.
马大为：她是我的朋友。

Jīn Lóng: Tā yě shì Níbó'ěrrén ma?
金龙：她也是尼泊尔人吗？

Mǎ Dàwéi: Bù, tā shì Zhōngguórén.
马大为：不，她是中国人。

Jin Long: Is this your book?
Ma Dawei: No, it's Li Zhen's book. Those are mine.
Jin Long: Who is Li Zhen?
Ma Dawei: She is my friend.
Jin Long: Is she a Nepalese, too?
Ma Dawei: No, she's a Chinese.

生词 New words

1.	这	zhè	pron.	this
2.	的	de	part.	used to indicate a possessive relationship
3.	书	shū	n.	book
4.	那些	nàxiē	pron.	those
	那	nà	pron.	that
5.	谁	shéi	pron.	who
6.	她	tā	pron.	she
7.	朋友	péngyou	n.	friend

第三课 你是哪国人？
Lesson 3 Where are you from?

专名 **Proper nouns**

1. 尼泊尔　　Níbó'ěr　　　　　Nepal
2. 中国　　　Zhōngguó　　　　China

语言点　Language Points

一、结构助词"的"　Structural particle "的"

结构助词"的"是定语的标志，用来连接定语和中心语。常见的结构是"定语＋的＋中心语"。例如：

The structural particle "的" is the sign of the attributive and is used to connect the attributive and the central word. The common structure is "attributive ＋ 的 ＋ central word". For example:

1. 你的书
2. 老师的名字
3. 我的朋友

如果定语是某人所属的国家，那么定语和中心语之间一般不用"的"。例如：

If the attributive is the country to which one belongs, "的" is usually not used between the attributive and the central word. For example:

4. 中国人
5. 中国老师
6. 尼泊尔学生
7. 泰国留学生

※ 练习：请用结构助词"的"完成对话　Please complete the dialogues with the structural particle "的"

1. A：这是你的书吗？
   B：_____。

2. A：李真是你的朋友吗？

　　B：_____。

3. A：_____？

　　B：不，他不是王晨的老师。

二、疑问代词"谁"　Interrogative pronoun "谁"

疑问代词"谁"用来询问人。例如：

The interrogative pronoun "谁" is used to ask about people. For example:

1. 谁是王老师？

2. 李真是谁？

3. 这是谁的书？

※ 练习：回答问题　Answer the questions

1. A：谁是你们的老师？

　　B：_____。

2. A：那是谁的书？

　　B：_____。

3. A：马大为是谁？

　　B：_____。

综合练习　Comprehensive Exercises

一、听录音，选出你听到的音节　Listen to the recording and pick out the syllables you hear

1. A. zé　　B. zhè
2. A. zhè　 B. chē
3. A. shū　 B. sū

4. A. zhū　 B. shū
5. A. shéi　B. suí
6. A. xuē　 B. xiē

第三课　你是哪国人？
Lesson 3　Where are you from?

二、根据汉字写拼音 Write Pinyin according to Chinese characters

1. 谁_____ 3. 那些_____ 5. 的_____

2. 这_____ 4. 书_____ 6. 朋友_____

三、朗读语句 Read aloud

1. 那些书
2. 这些书
3. 这些学生

4. 这些是谁的书?
5. 这些是我们的书。
6. 那些也是我们的书。

四、完成对话 Complete dialogues

金　龙：这是你的书吗?

马大为：_____，这是李真的书。_____些是我的书。

金　龙：李真是_____?

马大为：她是我_____朋友。

金　龙：她_____是尼泊尔人吗?

马大为：不，她是_____。

五、汉字书写 Write Chinese characters

这	辶 + 文	丶	一	亠	文	文	讠	这				
的	白 + 勺	丿	亻	白	白	白	白	的	的			
书		乛	乛	书	书							
她	女 + 也	𡿨	𡿨	女	女	如	如	她				

谁	讠+隹	、	讠	讣	计	计	许	许	谁	谁			
中		丶	口	口	中								

语言任务 Language Tasks

一、阅读理解 Reading comprehension

李真是马大为的朋友，她是中国人。美丽是南非人，金龙是泰国人，他们都是留学生。

读后判断 True or false

1. 李真认识马大为。　　　　　　　　　　　　　　　　　（　）
2. 李真是留学生。　　　　　　　　　　　　　　　　　　（　）
3. 美丽、金龙都不是中国人。　　　　　　　　　　　　　（　）

二、口头表达 Oral expression

任务名称：你是哪国人？

Task: Where are you from?

任务要求：两名学生一组，互相询问国籍。

Requirements: Work in pairs and ask each other's nationality.

Reference words: 哪国人　也　留学生　是　都

第四课 Lesson 4

Nǐ yǒu Zhōngguó péngyou ma?
你有 中国 朋友 吗?
Do you have Chinese friends?

学习目标 Learning Objectives

1. Language Function: Ask about other people's friends, family members or introduce your own friends and family members.
2. Language Points: Possession sentence — "有"-sentence; Adverb "真"; Interrogative pronoun "几"; Conjunction "和".

热身活动 Warming-up

1. 你有几个中国朋友?
How many Chinese friends do you have?

2. 你家有几口人?
How many people are there in your family?

课文（一）
Text (1)

(Li Zhen and Wang Chen are chatting on campus.)

Lǐ Zhēn: Nǐ yǒu wàiguó péngyou ma?
李真：你有外国朋友吗？

Wáng Chén: Wǒ yǒu hěn duō wàiguó péngyou.
王晨：我有很多外国朋友。

Lǐ Zhēn: Tāmen dōu shì nǎ guó rén?
李真：他们都是哪国人？

Wáng Chén: Hánguórén, Měiguórén, Fǎguórén.
王晨：韩国人、美国人、法国人。

Lǐ Zhēn: Nǐ de wàiguó péngyou zhēn duō!
李真：你的外国朋友真多！

Wáng Chén: Shì a, tāmen yě shì wǒ de tóngxué. Wǒmen yìqǐ xuéxí.
王晨：是啊，他们也是我的同学。我们一起学习。

Li Zhen: Do you have foreign friends?
Wang Chen: I have many foreign friends.
Li Zhen: Where are they from?
Wang Chen: They are Korean, American, and French.
Li Zhen: You have so many foreign friends!
Wang Chen: Yes! They are my classmates, too. We study together.

生词 New words

1. 有	yǒu	v.	to have
2. 外国	wàiguó	n.	foreign country
3. 多	duō	adj.	many, much
4. 他们	tāmen	pron.	they, them
5. 真	zhēn	adv./adj.	really; real
6. 啊	a	part.	a modal particle used at the end of a sentence to express affirmation

第四课 你有中国朋友吗？
Lesson 4 Do you have Chinese friends?

7. 同学	tóngxué	*n.*	classmate
8. 一起	yìqǐ	*adv.*	together
9. 学习	xuéxí	*v.*	to study

专名 Proper nouns

1. 韩国	Hánguó	Korea
2. 美国	Měiguó	America
3. 法国	Fǎguó	France

语言点 Language Points

一、表示领有的"有"字句　Possession sentence —"有"-sentence

"有"做谓语动词时，可以表示领有。例如：

When "有" acts as the predicate verb, it indicates possession. For example:

1. 我有很多朋友。

2. 马大为有很多同学。

3. 美丽有很多书。

表示否定时，一般在"有"的前面加"没（méi，not）"。例如：

In a negative sentence, "没 (méi, not) " is usually added before "有". For example:

4. 我没有外国朋友。

5. 马大为没有书。

※ 练习：回答问题 Answer the questions

1. A：你有书吗？
   B：＿＿＿＿＿＿＿＿＿＿＿＿＿。

2. A：你有中国老师吗？
   B：＿＿＿＿＿＿＿＿＿＿＿＿＿。

3. A：你有外国朋友吗？

B：_____。

二、副词"真" Adverb "真"

副词"真"表示的确、实在，有很强的感情色彩，常用在感叹句中。例如：

The adverb "真" means "really" and has strong emotion. It is often used in exclamatory sentences. For example:

1. 你的外国朋友真多！
2. 我们的老师真好！
3. 王晨的书真多！

※ 练习：请用副词"真"完成句子 Please complete the sentences with adverb "真"

1. 王晨的朋友_____！
2. 老师的书_____！
3. 他们的同学_____！

综合练习 Comprehensive Exercises

一、听录音，选出你听到的音节 Listen to the recording and pick out the syllables you hear

1. A. duō   B. tuō
2. A. shén   B. zhēn
3. A. wài   B. huài
4. A. qǐ   B. xǐ
5. A. yǒu   B. chǒu
6. A. yìqǐ   B. zìjǐ

二、根据汉字写拼音 Write Pinyin according to Chinese characters

1. 有_____   3. 一起_____   5. 学习_____
2. 外国_____ 4. 多_____   6. 同学_____

三、朗读语句 Read aloud

1. 你有中国朋友吗？
2. 我有很多中国朋友。
3. 我没有中国朋友。

4. 你的外国朋友真多！
5. 你们一起学习吗？
6. 我们一起学习。

四、完成对话 Complete dialogues

李真：你_____外国朋友吗？

王晨：我_____外国朋友。

李真：他们_____哪国人？

王晨：韩国人、美国人、法国人。

李真：你的外国朋友_____！

王晨：是啊，他们也是我的同学。我们_____。

五、汉字书写 Write Chinese characters

有	一	ナ	オ	ナ	有	有						
外	夕+卜											
	ノ	ク	タ	列	外							
真	十+具											
	一	十	卢	古	市	肯	肯	直	真	真		
多	夕+夕											
	ノ	ク	タ	夕	多	多						
起	走+己											
	一	十	士	丰	丰	丰	走	走	起	起		
习	冫	习	习									

课文（二）
Text (Ⅱ)

(Ma Dawei and Yueliang are chatting in the library.)

Mǎ Dàwéi: Yuèliang, nǐ xiǎng jiā ma?
马大为：月亮，你想家吗？

Yuèliang: Wǒ hěn xiǎng jiā.
月亮：我很想家。

Mǎ Dàwéi: Nǐ jiā yǒu jǐ kǒu rén?
马大为：你家有几口人？

Yuèliang: Wǒ jiā yǒu sān kǒu rén, bàba, māma hé wǒ. Wǒ xiǎng bàba māma,
月亮：我家有三口人，爸爸、妈妈和我。我想爸爸妈妈，
xiǎng wǒ de péngyou, yě xiǎng wǒ jiā de māo hé gǒu.
想我的朋友，也想我家的猫和狗。

Mǎ Dàwéi: Nǐ méiyǒu Zhōngguó péngyou ma?
马大为：你没有中国朋友吗？

Yuèliang: Wǒ méiyǒu Zhōngguó péngyou, nǐ ne?
月亮：我没有中国朋友，你呢？

Mǎ Dàwéi: Wǒ yǒu hěn duō Zhōngguó péngyou. Wǒ bù xiǎng jiā.
马大为：我有很多中国朋友。我不想家。

Ma Dawei: Yueliang, do you miss home?
Yueliang: Yes, I miss home very much.
Ma Dawei: How many people are there in your family?
Yueliang: There are three people in my family, my father, my mother and I. I miss my parents, my friends, and my kitten and doggie.
Ma Dawei: Don't you have Chinese friends?
Yueliang: I don't have Chinese friends, what about you?
Ma Dawei: I have many Chinese friends. I don't miss home.

生词 New words

1. 想　　　xiǎng　　　v.　　　to miss
2. 家　　　jiā　　　　n.　　　home, family

第四课　你有中国朋友吗？
Lesson 4　Do you have Chinese friends?

3. 几	jǐ	*pron.*	how many
4. 口	kǒu	*m.*	a measure word for family members, etc.
5. 三	sān	*num.*	three
6. 爸爸	bàba	*n.*	father, dad
7. 妈妈	māma	*n.*	mother, mom
8. 和	hé	*conj.*	and, with
9. 猫	māo	*n.*	cat
10. 狗	gǒu	*n.*	dog
11. 没有	méiyǒu	*v.*	there is not; to not have

专名 **Proper nouns**

月亮	Yuèliang	name of a Bahraini student

语言点 Language Points

一、疑问代词"几"　Interrogative pronoun "几"

疑问代词"几"一般用来询问10以下的数量,"几"后面的量词一般不能省略。例如:

The interrogative pronoun "几" is usually used to ask about quantities less than 10. The measure word after "几" usually cannot be omitted. For example:

1. A:你家有几口人?

   B:我家有三口人,爸爸、妈妈和我。

2. A:你有几个(gè, a measure word)老师?

   B:我有三个老师。

※ 练习:回答问题 Answer the questions

1. 你有几个中国朋友?

   _____。

2. 你有几个外国朋友？

    _____。

3. 金龙家有几口人？

    _____。

4. 月亮家有几口人？

    _____。

二、连词"和"　　Conjunction "和"

连词"和"表示并列关系，一般用来连接名词或代词。例如：

The conjunction "和" shows parallel relationship and is usually used to join nouns or pronouns. For example:

1. 老师和学生都是中国人。
2. 我家有猫和狗。
3. 我和他都是留学生。

如果连接三项或三项以上的成分，"和"要用在最后两项中间。例如：

If three or more components are joined, "和" should be used between the last two. For example:

4. 王晨、李真和美丽都是学生。
5. 金龙、美丽和月亮都是留学生。

※ 练习：请用连词"和"完成句子　Please complete the sentences with conjunction "和"

1. _____是学生。
2. _____也是我的同学。
3. _____都很高兴。

综合练习 Comprehensive Exercises

一、听录音，选出你听到的音节 Listen to the recording and pick out the syllables you hear

1. A. jiā   B. xiā
2. A. jǐ   B. qǐ
3. A. kǒu   B. gǒu

4. A. sān   B. shān
5. A. bà   B. pà
6. A. hé   B. huí

二、根据汉字写拼音 Write Pinyin according to Chinese characters

1. 和_____
2. 爸爸_____
3. 家_____
4. 狗_____
5. 妈妈_____
6. 想_____

三、朗读语句 Read aloud

1. 爸爸
2. 妈妈
3. 猫和狗

4. 你想爸爸和妈妈吗？
5. 我很想家。
6. 我也想我的朋友们。

四、完成对话 Complete dialogues

马大为：月亮，你想家吗？

月　亮：我很想家。

马大为：你家有_____人？

月　亮：我家有_____人，爸爸、妈妈_____我。我想爸爸妈妈，想_____，也想我家的猫_____狗。

马大为：你_____中国朋友吗？

月　亮：我没有中国朋友，你_____？

马大为：我有_____中国朋友。我不想家。

五、汉字书写 Write Chinese characters

想	相 + 心
几	
爸	父 + 巴
妈	女 + 马
和	禾 + 口
没	氵 + 殳

语言任务 Language Tasks

一、阅读理解 Reading comprehension

王晨有很多外国朋友，有韩国人、美国人和法国人。他们也是王晨的同学，和他一起学习。月亮没有中国朋友，她很想家，想爸爸妈妈，想她的朋友，也想她家的猫和狗。

读后判断 True or false

1. 王晨没有外国朋友。　　　　　　　　　　　　　　　　（　）
2. 月亮有很多中国朋友。　　　　　　　　　　　　　　　（　）
3. 月亮很想家。　　　　　　　　　　　　　　　　　　　（　）

二、口头表达 Oral expression

任务名称：你家有几口人？

Task: How many people are there in your family?

任务要求：两名学生一组，互相询问彼此的家庭情况。

Requirements: Work in pairs and ask about each other's families.

Reference words: 谁　家　有　口　爸爸　妈妈　和　想

第五课 Lesson 5

Wǒ yǒu wǔ gè wàiguó péngyou
我 有 五个 外国 朋友
I have five foreign friends

学习目标 Learning Objectives

1. Language Function: Express quantity and telephone number.
2. Language Points: Number expression in Chinese; Measure word "个"; Interrogative pronoun "多少"; Modal verb "可能"; Adverb "非常".

热身活动 Warming-up

1. 你的幸运数字是几?
   What is your lucky number?

2. 你知道下面这些手势在中国是什么意思吗?
   Do you know what these gestures mean in China?

课文（一）
Text（I）

(Wang Chen and his mom are chatting at home.)

māma: Nǐ yǒu jǐ gè wàiguó péngyou?
妈妈：你 有 几 个 外国 朋友？

Wáng Chén: Wǒ yǒu wǔ gè wàiguó péngyou.
王晨：我 有 五 个 外国 朋友。

māma: Tāmen dōu shì liúxuéshēng ma?
妈妈：他们 都 是 留学生 吗？

Wáng Chén: Duì, tāmen dōu shì yīxuéyuàn de liúxuéshēng.
王晨：对，他们 都 是 医学院 的 留学生。

māma: Yīxuéyuàn yǒu duōshao gè liúxuéshēng?
妈妈：医学院 有 多少 个 留学生？

Wáng Chén: Sānbǎi gè.
王晨：三百 个。

māma: Zhōngguó xuéshēng ne?
妈妈：中国 学生 呢？

Wáng Chén: Kěnéng yǒu liǎngqiān gè.
王晨：可能 有 两千 个。

Mom: How many foreign friends do you have?
Wang Chen: I have five foreign friends.
Mom: Are they all international students?
Wang Chen: Right, all of them are international students in the medical school.
Mom: How many international students are there in the medical school?
Wang Chen: 300.
Mom: How about Chinese students?
Wang Chen: Perhaps 2000.

生词 New words

1. 个	gè	*m.*	a measure word used before nouns without a special classifier of their own	
2. 五	wǔ	*num.*	five	

3. 医学院	yīxuéyuàn	n.	medical school
学院	xuéyuàn	n.	college, academy
4. 多少	duōshao	pron.	how many, how much
5. 百	bǎi	num.	hundred
6. 可能	kěnéng	mod.v.	perhaps, maybe, probably
7. 两	liǎng	num.	two
8. 千	qiān	num.	thousand

语言点 Language Points

一、汉语的数字表达法　Number expression in Chinese

0	1	2	3	4	5	6	7	8	9
líng	yī	èr	sān	sì	wǔ	liù	qī	bā	jiǔ
零	一	二	三	四	五	六	七	八	九
10	11	12	13	14	15	16	17	18	19
shí	shíyī	shí'èr	shísān	shísì	shíwǔ	shíliù	shíqī	shíbā	shíjiǔ
十	十一	十二	十三	十四	十五	十六	十七	十八	十九

20	21	22	23	24	25	26	27	28	29
èrshí	èrshíyī	··	èrshíjiǔ
二十	二十一	··	二十九

100	101	102	103	104	105	106	107	108	109
yìbǎi	yìbǎi líng yī	··	yìbǎi líng jiǔ
一百	一百零一	··	一百零九

110	111	112	113	··	119
yìbǎi yīshí	··	yìbǎi yīshíjiǔ
一百一十	··	一百一十九

1000
yìqiān
一千

※ 练习：请用汉字写出下列数字 Please write down the following numbers in Chinese

1. 37 _____

2. 99 _____

3. 206 _____

4. 300 _____

5. 320 _____

6. 1000 _____

二、量词"个" Measure word "个"

汉语的数词和名词中间一般要有量词，表示人或事物的数量单位。基本的结构是"数词＋量词＋名词"。汉语中有很多量词，其中"个"是一个很常见的量词。例如：

There is always a measure word between the numeral and the noun in Chinese, which represents the quantitative units of people or things. The basic structure is "numeral + measure word + noun". There are many measure words in Chinese, among which "个" is a very common one. For example:

1. 一个人

2. 两个朋友

3. 三个老师

4. 四个留学生

注意："二"一般不与普通量词连用，包括"个"；与普通量词连用时，前面一般要用"两"。

Attention: "两" is usually used with common measure words, including "个", instead of "二".

※ 练习：请给"个"找位置 Please find a place for "个"

1. 我 A 有 B 三 C 中国 D 朋友。　　　_____

2. A 医学院 B 有三百 C 留学生 D。　　_____

3. A 我有 B 两 C 老师 D。　　　　　_____

三、疑问代词"多少"　　Interrogative pronoun "多少"

疑问代词"多少"一般用来询问10以上的数量。"多少"后面的量词可以省略。例如：

The interrogative pronoun "多少" is used to ask about quantities of more than 10. The measure word after "多少" can be omitted. For example:

1. A：你们学院有多少（个）老师？
   B：我们学院有三十个老师。

2. A：你有多少（个）中国朋友？
   B：我有很多中国朋友。

3. A：医学院有多少（个）留学生？
   B：三百个。

※ 练习：回答问题　Answer the questions

1. 你有多少（个）中国朋友？
   ＿＿＿＿＿＿＿＿＿＿＿＿＿＿＿。

2. 你有多少（个）同学？
   ＿＿＿＿＿＿＿＿＿＿＿＿＿＿＿。

3. 你认识多少（个）留学生？
   ＿＿＿＿＿＿＿＿＿＿＿＿＿＿＿。

四、能愿动词"可能"　　Modal verb "可能"

能愿动词"可能"表示估计、推测，用在主语后、动词前。例如：

The modal verb "可能" is used between the subject and the verb to indicate estimation or speculation. For example:

1. A：医学院有多少（个）中国学生？
   B：可能有两千个。

2. 金龙可能是泰国人。

3. 他家可能有五口人。

※ 练习：请用能愿动词"可能"回答问题 Please answer the questions with modal verb "可能"

1. 这是谁的书？
   _____。

2. 马大为家有几口人？
   _____。

3. 你们学院有多少（个）中国学生？
   _____。

综合练习 Comprehensive Exercises

一、听录音，选出你听到的音节 Listen to the recording and pick out the syllables you hear

1. A. gè   B. kè
2. A. néng   B. lěng
3. A. sān   B. cān
4. A. shǎo   B. sǎo
5. A. bǎi   B. pài
6. A. qiān   B. xiàn

二、根据汉字写拼音 Write Pinyin according to Chinese characters

1. 个_____   3. 多少_____   5. 两_____
2. 百_____   4. 五_____   6. 可能_____

三、朗读语句 Read aloud

1. 三百个中国学生
2. 五百个留学生
3. 两千个学生

4. 医学院有多少个学生？
5. 可能有三千个。
6. 有五千个学生。

四、完成对话 Complete dialogues

妈妈：你有_____外国朋友？

王晨：我有五个外国朋友。

妈妈：他们_____留学生吗？

王晨：对，他们都是_____的留学生。

妈妈：医学院有_____留学生？

王晨：三_____个。

妈妈：中国学生_____？

王晨：_____有两千个。

五、汉字书写 Write Chinese characters

千	丿	二	千							
个	丿	人	个							
五	一	丆	五	五						
两	一	厂	兯	丙	丙	两	两			
百	一	丆	丆	百	百	百				
少	丨	丷	小	少						

课文（二）
Text (Ⅱ)

(Wang Chen and Ma Dawei are chatting in the dining room.)

Wáng Chén: Nǐmen sùshè yǒu diànhuà ma?
王晨：   你们 宿舍 有 电话 吗？

Mǎ Dàwéi: Yǒu.
马大为：有。

Wáng Chén: Diànhuà hàomǎ shì shénme?
王晨：   电话 号码 是 什么？

Mǎ Dàwéi: 83274695.　Nǐ de diànhuà hàomǎ shì shénme?
马大为：83274695。你 的 电话 号码 是 什么？

Wáng Chén: Wǒmen sùshè méiyǒu diànhuà, wǒ de shǒujī hàomǎ shì 13826668866.
王晨：   我们 宿舍 没有 电话，我的 手机 号码 是 13826668866。

Mǎ Dàwéi: Yǒu hěn duō liù hé bā.
马大为：有 很 多 六 和 八。

Wáng Chén: Duì ya, Zhōngguórén fēicháng xǐhuan liù hé bā.
王晨：   对呀， 中国人 非常 喜欢 六 和 八。

Mǎ Dàwéi: Wǒ xǐhuan jiǔ!
马大为：我 喜欢 九！

Wang Chen: Is there a phone in your dormitory?
Ma Dawei: Yes.
Wang Chen: What is the phone number?
Ma Dawei: 83274695. And yours?
Wang Chen: Our dormitory doesn't have a phone. My cellphone number is 13826668866.
Ma Dawei: There are many 6 and 8.
Wang Chen: Yes, Chinese people extremely like 6 and 8.
Ma Dawei: I like 9!

生词 New words

1. 宿舍	sùshè	n.	dormitory
2. 电话	diànhuà	n.	phone

3. 号码	hàomǎ	n.	number
4. 手机	shǒujī	n.	cellphone
5. 六	liù	num.	six
6. 八	bā	num.	eight
7. 呀	ya	part.	a modal particle used at the end of a sentence to express affirmation, like 啊
8. 非常	fēicháng	adv.	very, extremely
9. 喜欢	xǐhuan	v.	to like
10. 九	jiǔ	num.	nine

语言点 Language Points

副词"非常"　Adverb "非常"

副词"非常"表示程度高，常用在形容词和心理动词前。例如：

The adverb "非常" indicates high degree and is often used before adjectives and mental verbs. For example:

1. 马大为的中国朋友非常多。

2. 中国人非常喜欢六和八。

3. 月亮非常想家。

※ 练习：请用副词"非常"完成句子　Please complete the sentences with adverb "非常"

1. 你好！认识你_____。

2. 老师的书_____。

3. 月亮_____她家的猫和狗。

第五课　我有五个外国朋友
Lesson 5　I have five foreign friends

综合练习 Comprehensive Exercises

一、听录音，选出你听到的音节 Listen to the recording and pick out the syllables you hear

1. A. sù   B. shù
2. A. shè   B. sè
3. A. mā   B. mǎ

4. A. liù   B. jiǔ
5. A. huā   B. huān
6. A. jiǔ   B. xiǔ

二、根据汉字写拼音 Write Pinyin according to Chinese characters

1. 宿舍_____   3. 非常_____   5. 手机_____
2. 号码_____   4. 电话_____   6. 喜欢_____

三、朗读语句 Read aloud

1. 电话号码
2. 手机号码
3. 打（dǎ, to dial）电话

4. 我非常喜欢六和八。
5. 我不喜欢三和五。
6. 你的电话号码是什么？

四、完成对话 Complete dialogues

王　晨：你们宿舍有电话吗？

马大为：有。

王　晨：电话_____是什么？

马大为：83274695。你的电话号码是什么？

王　晨：我们宿舍_____电话，我的_____号码是13826668866。

马大为：有_____六和八。

王　晨：对呀，中国人_____喜欢六和八。

马大为：我喜欢九！

五、汉字书写 Write Chinese characters

宿	宀 + 佰	丶	宀	宀	宀	宀	宀	宀	宿	宿		
舍	人 + 舌	丿	人	人	스	全	仐	舍	舍			
电		丶	口	曰	日	电						
话	讠 + 舌	丶	讠	讠	讠	讠	讠	话	话			
非	丨 + 卝	丨	丨	丨	丰	非	非	非	非			
常	丷 + 吊	丨	丨	丷	丷	兴	兴	常	常	常	常	

语言任务 Language Tasks

一、阅读理解 Reading comprehension

　　王晨有五个外国朋友，他们都是医学院的留学生。医学院有三百个留学生、两千个中国学生。

读后判断 True or false

1. 王晨有六个外国朋友。　　　　　　　　　　　　　　（　）
2. 医学院有五百个留学生。　　　　　　　　　　　　　（　）
3. 医学院没有中国学生。　　　　　　　　　　　　　　（　）

二、口头表达 Oral expression

任务名称：你的电话/手机号码是什么？

Task: What's your phone/cellphone number?

任务要求：两名学生一组，互相询问彼此的电话/手机号码。

Requirements: Work in pairs and ask each other for their phone/cellphone numbers.

Reference words: 多少　电话号码　手机号码　喜欢

第六课 Lesson 6

Jīntiān jǐ yuè jǐ hào?
今天几月几号?
What's the date today?

学习目标 Learning Objectives

1. Language Function: Express date and age.
2. Language Points: Expressions for date; Expressions for age; Noun predicate sentence; Time noun "时候"; Modal particle "吧" (1).

热身活动 Warming-up

1. 你知道图片上的这位女士是谁吗？你听说过她的什么事迹吗？
   Do you know the lady in the following picture? Have you heard any story about her?

2. 中国最重要的节日是什么？
   What is the most important festival in China?

课文（一）
Text（I）

(Jin Long and Meili are chatting in the classroom.)

Jīn Lóng: Tiānqì zhēn hǎo!
金龙：天气 真 好！

Měilì: Duì, bù lěng yě bú rè.
美丽：对，不冷也不热。

Jīn Lóng: Jīntiān jǐ yuè jǐ hào?
金龙：今天 几月几号？

Měilì: Wǔ yuè shí'èr hào.
美丽：五 月 十二 号。

Jīn Lóng: Jīntiān shì yí gè zhòngyào de jiérì.
金龙：今天 是一个 重要 的节日。

Měilì: Shénme jiérì?
美丽：什么 节日？

Jīn Lóng: Hùshi Jié!
金龙：护士节。

Měilì: Duì! Wǔ yuè shí'èr rì shì Hùshi Jié!
美丽：对！五 月 十二 日是护士节！

Jin Long: The weather is really nice today.

Meili: Yes, neither cold nor hot.

Jin Long: What's the date today?

Meili: May 12th.

Jin Long: Today is an important festival.

Meili: What festival?

Jin Long: Nurses' Day!

Meili: Right! May 12th is Nurses' Day!

生词 New words

1. 天气	tiānqì	*n.*	weather
天	tiān	*n.*	sky, weather
2. 冷	lěng	*adj.*	cold

3. 热	rè	adj.	hot
4. 今天	jīntiān	n.	today
天	tiān	m.	day
5. 月	yuè	n.	month
6. 号	hào	m.	date
7. 十二	shí'èr	num.	twelve
十	shí	num.	ten
二	èr	num.	two
8. 重要	zhòngyào	adj.	important
9. 节日	jiérì	n.	festival
节	jié	n.	festival
日	rì		a certain day
10. 护士	hùshi	n.	nurse
11. 日	rì	n.	day

专名 Proper nouns

| 护士节 | Hùshi Jié | | Nurses' Day |

语言点 Language Points

日期表达法　Expressions for date

在汉语中，我们一般用"×月×日"或"×月×号"来表达日期。例如，"October 20th"可以读作"十月二十日"或"十月二十号"。

In Chinese, the date is expressed in the form of "×月×日" or "×月×号". For example, "October 20th" is read as "十月二十日" or "十月二十号".

表达月份是：

The expressions for months are:

一月　二月　三月　四月　五月　六月

七月　八月　九月　十月　十一月　十二月

表达某一天是：

第六课　今天几月几号？
Lesson 6　What's the date today?

The expressions for a day are:

一日/号　二日/号　三日/号……三十一日/号

询问日期时，我们一般用"……几月几号？"。例如：

"……几月几号？" is the common way of asking date. For example:

A：今天几月几号？

B：（今天）五月十二号。

※ 练习：请用汉字写出下列日期 Please write down the following dates in Chinese

1. 6th July
   _____

2. 5月12日
   _____

3. 9月6号
   _____

综合练习 Comprehensive Exercises

一、根据汉字写拼音 Write Pinyin according to Chinese characters

1. 今天_____　　3. 热_____　　5. 号_____

2. 冷_____　　　4. 重要_____　6. 月_____

二、朗读语句 Read aloud

1. 今天一月一号。
2. 今天天气真好！
3. 今天天气不冷也不热。
4. 她是护士。
5. 今天是护士节。
6. 今天是一个重要的节日。

三、替换练习 Substitution drills

1. 天气真 好！

2. 不 冷 也不 热。

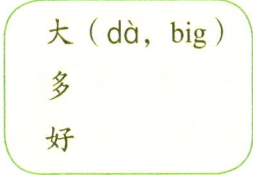

3. 今天是 五 月 十二 号。

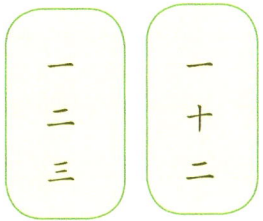

四、选词填空 Use the following words to fill in the blanks

号　真　护士　重要　热

1. 天气很_____。

2. 马大为的妈妈是一个_____。

3. 今天的天气_____好！

4. 护士节是几月几_____？

5. 十月一日是中国的一个_____节日。

五、根据课文内容回答问题 Answer the following questions according to the text

1. 今天天气好吗?

2. 今天几月几号?

3. 今天是什么节日?

六、根据课文内容填空 Fill in the blanks according to the text

金龙问（wèn, to ask）美丽今天是几_____几_____，美丽告诉（gàosu, to tell）金龙今天是五月十二号，是一个非常_____的节日——_____节。

七、汉字书写 Write Chinese characters

月	ノ	刀	月	月					
日	丨	冂	日	日					
天	一	二	于	天					
气	ノ	⺊	⺧	气					
今	ノ	人	亼	今					
冷	冫+令　丶	冫	冫	冫	冷	冷	冷		

课文（二）
Text（Ⅱ）

(Jin Long and Wang Chen are chatting in the classroom.)

Wáng Chén: Jīn Lóng, nǐ jīnnián duō dà?
王晨：金龙，你今年多大？

Jīn Lóng: Wǒ jīnnián èrshíyī suì, nǐ ne?
金龙：我今年二十一岁，你呢？

Wáng Chén: Wǒ shíjiǔ suì. Nǐ de shēngrì shì jǐ yuè jǐ hào?
王晨：我十九岁。你的生日是几月几号？

Jīn Lóng: Sì yuè qī hào.
金龙：四月七号。

Wáng Chén: Nǐ guò shēngrì de shíhou, wǒmen yìqǐ chīfàn ba.
王晨：你过生日的时候，我们一起吃饭吧。

Jīn Lóng: Hǎo. Nǐ de shēngrì shì jǐ yuè jǐ hào?
金龙：好。你的生日是几月几号？

Wáng Chén: Wǒ de shēngrì shì yí gè zhòngyào de jiérì!
王晨：我的生日是一个重要的节日！

Jīn Lóng: Shénme jiérì?
金龙：什么节日？

Wáng Chén: Yuándàn!
王晨：元旦！

Wang Chen: Jin Long, how old are you?
Jin Long: I'm 21 years old, and you?
Wang Chen: I'm 19 years old. When is your birthday?
Jin Long: April 7th.
Wang Chen: Let's eat together on your birthday.
Jin Long: OK. When is your birthday?
Wang Chen: My birthday is on an important festival!
Jin Long: What festival?
Wang Chen: New Year's Day!

生词 New words

1.	今年	jīnnián	n.	this year
	年	nián	n.	year
2.	多	duō	pron.	used to ask degree or quantity in interrogative sentences
3.	大	dà	adj.	old, big
4.	二十一	èrshíyī	num.	twenty-one
	一	yī	num.	one
5.	岁	suì	m.	year (of age)
6.	生日	shēngrì	n.	birthday
7.	四	sì	num.	four
8.	七	qī	num.	seven
9.	过	guò	v.	to spend (time)
10.	时候	shíhou	n.	time
11.	吃饭	chīfàn	v.	to have a meal
	吃	chī	v.	to eat
	饭	fàn	n.	meal
12.	吧	ba	part.	used at the end of a sentence to indicate a mild suggestion
13.	好	hǎo	adj.	used to express approval or agreement

专名 Proper nouns

元旦	Yuándàn		New Year's Day

语言点 Language Points

一、年龄表达法　Expressions for age

在汉语中，我们用数词加"岁"表示年龄。例如：

In Chinese, age is expressed by the form of "numerals ＋ 岁". For example:

1. 他十八岁。

2. 马大为二十岁。

3. 王老师今年四十六岁。

询问年龄的时候，我们一般用"你（今年）多大？"。

When asking for age, we usually raise the question "你（今年）多大？".

如果询问的是10岁以下的儿童，我们常用"你（今年）几岁？"。

If asking a child under 10 years old, we usually raise the question "你（今年）几岁？".

※ 练习：回答问题 Answer the questions

1. 你今年多大？

_____。

2. 你的好朋友今年多大？

_____。

3. 月亮的猫今年几岁？

_____。

二、名词谓语句　Noun predicate sentence

在汉语中，部分名词、名词性短语或数量短语可以做谓语，表示日期、年龄、价格、天气、籍贯等。例如：

In Chinese, some nouns, nominal phrases or quantitative phrases can be used as a predicate, indicating date, age, price, weather, place of birth, etc. For example:

1. 今天八月八号。

2. 王老师三十七岁。

3. 这个手机两千元（yuán, currency unit of RMB）。

4. 今天天气三十八度（dù, calibration）。

5. 王晨北京（Běijīng, Beijing）人。

※ 练习：完成对话 Complete dialogues

1. A：今天几月几号？

第六课　今天几月几号？
Lesson 6　What's the date today?

B：_____。

2. A：_____？

　　B：我今年四十岁。

3. A：王老师今年多大？

　　B：_____。

三、时间名词"时候"　　Time noun "时候"

时间名词"时候"常用在结构"……的时候"里表示时间。例如：

The time noun "时候" is often used in the construction "……的时候". For example:

1. 过生日的时候，我们一起吃饭。

2. 吃饭的时候，我很高兴。

3. 元旦的时候，我过生日。

在疑问句中，它前面常跟"什么"搭配来询问时间。例如：

In an interrogative sentence, it's often paired with "什么" to ask the time. For example:

4. 你什么时候过生日？

5. 我们什么时候吃饭？

6. 你什么时候学习汉语？

※ 练习：完成对话 Complete dialogues

1. A：你什么时候过生日？

　　B：_____。

2. A：过生日的时候，你喜欢吃什么？

　　B：_____。

3. A：你什么时候和朋友一起吃饭？

　　B：_____。

四、语气助词"吧"（1）　　Modal particle "吧"（1）

语气助词"吧"用在句尾，可以表示建议或者请求。例如：

The modal particle "吧" is used at the end of a sentence to suggest or request. For example:

1. 过生日的时候，我们一起吃饭吧。

2. 今年我们一起过元旦吧！

3. 明天（míngtiān，tomorrow）我们一起学习吧。

※ 练习：请用语气助词"吧"和所给词语完成下列对话　Please complete the following dialogues with modal particle "吧" and the words given

1. A：马大为过生日的时候，我们做（zuò，to do）什么？
　　B：_____。（吃饭）

2. A：今天我们吃什么？
　　B：_____。（火锅，huǒguō，hot pot）

3. A：元旦我们做（zuò，to do）什么？
　　B：_____。（看电影，kàn diànyǐng，see a movie）

综合练习 Comprehensive Exercises

一、根据汉字写拼音 Write Pinyin according to Chinese characters

1. 生日_____　　3. 年_____　　5. 过_____

2. 时候_____　　4. 吃饭_____　6. 岁_____

二、朗读语句 Read aloud

1. 过生日
2. 一起吃饭
3. 七月四号
4. 你今年多大？
5. 我今年二十一岁。
6. 我的生日是一个重要的节日。

三、替换练习 Substitution drills

1. 你今年多大？我今年 二十一 岁。

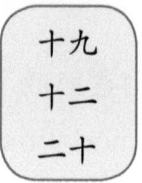

十九
十二
二十

2. 我二十一岁，你 呢？

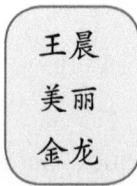

王晨
美丽
金龙

3. 我的生日是 一个重要的节日。

四月七号
护士节，五月十二号
元旦，一月一号

四、选词填空 Use the following words to fill in the blanks

大　时候　过　岁　吃饭

1. 你多_____？

2. 你几_____？

3. 我今天_____生日。

4. 我们一起_____吧。

5. 你的生日是什么_____？

五、根据课文内容回答问题 Answer the following questions according to the text

1. 金龙今年多大?
2. 王晨今年多大?
3. 金龙的生日是几月几号?
4. 王晨的生日是什么节日?

六、根据课文内容填空 Fill in the blanks according to the text

金龙今年＿＿＿＿＿＿＿，王晨＿＿＿＿＿＿＿。金龙的生日是四＿＿＿＿＿＿＿七＿＿＿＿＿＿＿。金龙＿＿＿＿＿＿＿生日的＿＿＿＿＿＿＿，王晨想和金龙＿＿＿＿＿＿＿吃饭。王晨的生日是一个重要的＿＿＿＿＿＿＿——元旦。

七、汉字书写 Write Chinese characters

吃	口 + 乞									
	丨	口	口	吖	吃					
饭	饣 + 反									
	丿	𠂉	饣	忆	饣	饭	饭			
年	丿	⺊	乍	𠂈	年					
岁	山 + 夕									
	丨	山	山	少	岁	岁				
过	辶 + 寸									
	一	十	寸	寸	讨	过				
吧	口 + 巴									
	丨	口	口	吅	吧	吧				

第六课 今天几月几号?
Lesson 6 What's the date today?

语言任务 Language Tasks

一、阅读理解 Reading comprehension

今天是护士节，也是美丽的生日。美丽今年十九岁。金龙和王晨是美丽的朋友。金龙今年二十一岁，他的生日是四月七号。王晨今年十九岁，他的生日是一个很重要的节日——元旦。

读后判断 True or false

1. 护士节是美丽的生日。　　　　　　　　　　　　　　　　　（　）
2. 金龙今年十九岁。　　　　　　　　　　　　　　　　　　　（　）
3. 王晨的生日是一个很重要的节日。　　　　　　　　　　　　（　）

二、口头表达 Oral expression

任务名称：了解朋友的年龄和生日。

Task: Find out your friend's age and birthday.

任务要求：1. 三名学生一组，互相询问彼此的生日。

　　　　　2. 三名学生一起完成表格。

Requirements: 1. Work in groups of three and ask each other about their birthdays.

　　　　　　　2. Three students complete the table together.

Reference words: 多　大　月　日　生日　重要　节日　岁　一起　吃饭

我们的生日

Number	Name	Age	Birthday
学生1			
学生2			
学生3			

第七课 Lesson 7

Wǒmen bā diǎn shàngkè
我们 八点 上课
We start class at 8 o'clock

学习目标 Learning Objectives

1. Language Function: Ask or express time.
2. Language Points: Expressions for time (1) (2) (3); Adverb "就" (1); Locative noun "前"; Exclamatory sentence "太……了".

热身活动 Warming-up

1. 你们一般几点起床？几点睡觉？
   What time do you usually get up and go to sleep?

2. 你们几点上课？几点下课？
   What time do you start and finish your class?

85

课文（一）
Text (I)

(Wang Chen and Li Zhen are chatting in the dining room.)

Wáng Chén: Nǐmen zǎoshang jǐ diǎn shàngkè?
王晨：你们 早上 几点 上课？

Lǐ Zhēn: Bā diǎn shàngkè.
李真：八 点 上课。

Wáng Chén: Jǐ diǎn xiàkè?
王晨：几点 下课？

Lǐ Zhēn: Zhōngwǔ shíyī diǎn sìshí fēn xiàkè.
李真：中午 十一 点 四十分 下课。

Wáng Chén: Nǐmen xiàwǔ yǒu kè ma?
王晨：你们 下午有 课吗？

Lǐ Zhēn: Yǒu.
李真：有。

Wáng Chén: Wǒmen xiàwǔ méiyǒu kè.
王晨：我们 下午没有 课。

Lǐ Zhēn: Nǐ xiàwǔ zuò shénme?
李真：你 下午 做 什么？

Wáng Chén: Dúshū, xiě zuòyè, wánr diànnǎo yóuxì.
王晨：读书，写 作业，玩儿 电脑 游戏。

Wang Chen: When does your class begin in the morning?
    Li Zhen: We start class at eight o'clock.
Wang Chen: What time is the class over?
    Li Zhen: Eleven forty in the morning.
Wang Chen: Do you have classes in the afternoon?
    Li Zhen: Yes, we have.
Wang Chen: We don't have classes in the afternoon.
    Li Zhen: What do you do in the afternoon?
Wang Chen: Reading, doing homework and playing computer games.

生词 New words

1. 早上	zǎoshang	n.	morning
早	zǎo	n./adj.	morning; early
2. 点	diǎn	m.	o'clock
3. 上课	shàngkè	v.	to go to class
课	kè	n.	class, lesson
4. 下课	xiàkè	v.	to finish class
5. 中午	zhōngwǔ	n.	noon
6. 分	fēn	m.	minute
7. 下午	xiàwǔ	n.	afternoon
8. 做	zuò	v.	to do
9. 读书	dúshū	v.	to read, to study
读	dú	v.	to read
10. 写	xiě	v.	to write
11. 作业	zuòyè	n.	homework
12. 玩儿	wánr	v.	to play
13. 电脑	diànnǎo	n.	computer
14. 游戏	yóuxì	n.	game

语言点 Language Points

时间表达法（1） Expressions for time (1)

汉语一般用"点"和"分"来表示时间。例如：

"点" and "分" are used in Chinese to indicate time. For example:

8：00　八点

8：05　八点零五（分）

8：10　八点十分

8：25　八点二十五（分）

8：56　八点五十六（分）

第七课　我们八点上课

Lesson 7　We start class at 8 o'clock

注意： 当表示"分"的数字是单音节"十"时，"分"不能省略。例如8：10，我们不能读作"八点十"，而要说"八点十分"。当表示"分"的数字是单音节"一"到"九"时，"分"也不能省略；如要省略"分"，我们可以在数字前加"零"，使之变成双音节。例如8：05，我们可以读作"八点五分"，也可以读作"八点零五"。当表示"分"的数字是双音节或更多音节时，"分"在口语中可以省略。例如8：25，我们既可以读作"八点二十五分"，也可以读作"八点二十五"。

Attention: When the number before "分" is the single-syllable "十", "分" cannot be omitted. For example, 8：10 should be read as "八点十分", instead of "八点十". When the number before "分" is the single-syllable "一" to "九", "分" also cannot be omitted either. The speaker could add "零" in front of the single-syllable number to make it a disyllable. For example, 8：05 can be read as "八点五分" or "八点零五". "分" can be omitted in spoken Chinese when the number before it is a disyllable or multi-syllable. For example, 8：25 can be read as "八点二十五分" or "八点二十五".

询问时间时，一般用"现在几点？"。

"现在几点？" is often used to ask the time.

时间名词"今天、早上、中午、下午"等一般要放在具体时间的前面。例如：

Time nouns, such as "今天、早上、中午、下午", are usually put in front of the specific time. For example:

今天早上八点上课。

今天中午十二点下课。

今天下午三点没有课。

时间词做状语时一般放在动词的前面。例如：

When a time noun is used as an adverbial modifier, it is usually placed before the verb. For example:

今天八点上课。

下午四点下课。

今天下午五点吃饭。

※ 练习：请用汉字写出下列时间 Please write down the following time in Chinese

1. 5：20 a.m.

   _____

2. 4：10 p.m.

   _____

3. 9：40 a.m.

   _____

4. 3：29 p.m.

   _____

5. 2：30 p.m.

   _____

6. 6：02 a.m.

   _____

综合练习 Comprehensive Exercises

一、根据汉字写拼音 Write Pinyin according to Chinese characters

1. 点_____   3. 上课_____   5. 中午_____

2. 早上_____ 4. 做_____   6. 作业_____

二、朗读语句 Read aloud

1. 早上八点。
2. 今天没有课。
3. 我下午有课。
4. 你们几点下课？
5. 你下午上课吗？
6. 你下午做什么？

第七课　我们八点上课

Lesson 7　We start class at 8 o'clock

三、替换练习 Substitution drills

1. 你们几点 上课?

   下课
   写作业
   吃饭

2. 你们 下午 有课吗?

   今天
   早上
   中午

3. 我 中午 十一点四十分 下课。

   早上　　九点四十五分
   中午　　十二点十分
   下午　　两点五十分

四、选词填空 Use the following words to fill in the blanks

点　做　玩儿　上课　写

1. 我很喜欢_____汉字（Hànzì, character）。

2. 你喜欢_____游戏吗?

3. 医学院早上几点_____?

4. 你今天下午_____什么?

5. 你中午几_____下课?

五、根据课文内容回答问题 Answer the following questions according to the text

1. 李真早上几点上课？

2. 李真中午几点下课？

3. 王晨下午有课吗？

4. 王晨下午做什么？

六、根据课文内容填空 Fill in the blanks according to the text

李真_____八点上课，_____十一点四十分下课。她下午也有课。王晨下午_____课，他下午_____，_____，玩儿_____。

七、汉字书写 Write Chinese characters

早	日 + 十
	丶 丨 口 曰 日 旦 早
上	丨 卜 上
下	一 丅 下
分	八 + 刀
	丿 八 分 分
午	丿 ⺍ 二 午
做	亻 + 故
	丿 亻 亻 什 什 估 估 估 做 做

课文（二）
Text (Ⅱ)

(Yueliang and Meili are chatting in the dormitory.)

Yuèliang: Xiànzài jǐ diǎn?
月亮：现在几点？

Měilì: Chà yí kè shí'èr diǎn.
美丽：差一刻十二点。

Yuèliang: Tài wǎn le, shuìjiào ba. Míngtiān zǎoshang liù diǎn bàn jiù qǐchuáng, bā diǎn qián dào jiàoshì.
月亮：太晚了，睡觉吧。明天早上六点半就起床，八点前到教室。

Měilì: Míngtiān méiyǒu kè.
美丽：明天没有课。

Yuèliang: Wèi shénme méiyǒu kè?
月亮：为什么没有课？

Měilì: Míngtiān xīngqī jǐ?
美丽：明天星期几？

Yuèliang: Xīngqī…
月亮：星期……

Měilì: Xīngqīliù.
美丽：星期六。

Yuèliang: Méiyǒu kè! Tài hǎo le!
月亮：没有课！太好了！

Yueliang: What time is it now?

Meili: A quarter to twelve.

Yueliang: It's too late. Time to go to sleep. We need to get up at six thirty tomorrow morning and arrive at the classroom before eight.

Meili: We don't have class tomorrow.

Yueliang: Why don't we have class?

Meili: What day is it tomorrow?

Yueliang: It's…

Meili: It's Saturday.

Yueliang: No class! That's great!

生词 New words

1. 现在	xiànzài	n.	now
2. 差	chà	v.	to be short of
3. 刻	kè	m.	quarter
4. 太……了	tài…le		too, extremely
太	tài	adv.	extremely
5. 晚	wǎn	adj.	late
6. 睡觉	shuìjiào	v.	to go to bed
7. 明天	míngtiān	n.	tomorrow
8. 半	bàn	num.	half
9. 就	jiù	adv.	as early as
10. 起床	qǐchuáng	v.	to get up
11. 前	qián	n.	before
12. 到	dào	v.	to arrive
13. 教室	jiàoshì	n.	classroom
14. 为什么	wèi shénme		why
15. 星期	xīngqī	n.	week
16. 星期六	xīngqīliù	n.	Saturday

语言点 Language Points

一、时间表达法（2）　Expressions for time (2)

汉语也常常用"半"和"刻"来表示时间。例如：

In Chinese, "半" and "刻" are often used to express time. For example:

8：15　八点一刻 / 八点十五（分）

8：30　八点半 / 八点三十（分）

8：45　八点三刻 / 差一刻九点 / 八点四十五（分）

第七课　我们八点上课

Lesson 7　We start class at 8 o'clock

※ 练习：请用汉字写出下列时间　Please write down the following time in Chinese

1. 10：15 a.m.
   _____

2. 5：30 p.m.
   _____

3. 7：45 a.m.
   _____

4. 3：30 a.m.
   _____

二、副词"就"（1）　Adverb "就" (1)

副词"就"常用在具体时间之后、动词之前，表示事情发生的时间早。例如：

The adverb "就" is often used between the special time and the verb to indicate that something happens early. For example:

1. 明天早上六点半就起床。
2. 下午四点半就吃饭。
3. 九点就睡觉。

※ 练习：请用副词"就"回答问题　Please answer the questions with adverb "就"

1. 你早上几点起床？
   _____。

2. 你几点吃早饭（zǎofàn，breakfast）？
   _____。

3. 你们早上几点上课？
   _____。

4. 你几点睡觉？
   _____。

三、方位名词 "前"　　Locative noun "前"

方位名词 "前" 可以用在名词、数量词、动词后表示时间。例如：

The locative noun "前" can be used after nouns, quantifiers, and verbs to indicate time. For example:

1. 我们中午前到医学院。

2. 我们八点前到教室。

3. 我六点前就起床。

4. 我们上课前吃饭。

※　练习：请用方位名词 "前" 回答问题　Please answer the questions with locative noun "前"

1. 你明天几点起床？

　　_____。

2. 你什么时候吃早饭？

　　_____。

3. 你几点睡觉？

　　_____。

4. 你明天几点到教室？

　　_____。

四、时间表达法（3）　　Expressions for time (3)

汉语一般用 "星期×" 表示星期。例如：

In Chinese, "星期×" is used to express the day of a week. For example:

星期一	Monday	星期五	Friday
星期二	Tuesday	星期六	Saturday
星期三	Wednesday	星期日/星期天	Sunday
星期四	Thursday		

询问星期，一般用 "……星期几？"。例如：

The question "……星期几？" is usually used to ask about the day of a week. For example:

1. A：今天星期几？

   B：今天星期六。

2. A：明天星期几？

   B：明天星期日。

星期表达和日期表达可以结合起来，其表达形式为"×月×日/号星期×"。例如：

Week expressions can be combined with date expressions, the expression form should be "×月×日/号星期×". For example:

一月一日星期六

八月八号星期五

星期表达也可以和时间表达结合起来，例如：

Week expressions can also be combined with time expressions. For example:

星期一上午八点半

星期六下午六点三十分

※ 练习：回答问题 Answer the questions

1. 今天星期三，明天星期几？

   _____。

2. 今年的五月十二号是星期几？

   _____。

3. 今年你的生日是星期几？

   _____。

4. 你喜欢星期几？

   _____。

五、感叹句"太……了"　Exclamatory sentence "太……了"

感叹句"太……了"表示强烈的感情，中间的成分常常是形容词或心理动词。具体又分为两种情况：

The exclamatory sentence "太……了" expresses strong feelings. The central component is often an adjective or a mental verb. There are specifically two cases:

一种情况是：表示程度过高，超出了说话人的主观预期，多用于不满意的事情。例如：

In one case, the degree is so high that it is beyond the speaker's subjective expectations. It is often used when the speaker is not satisfied. For example:

1. 十二点睡觉，太晚了！
2. 今天天气太冷了！
3. 中午天气太热了！
4. 你太喜欢玩儿游戏了，这不好。

另一种情况是：表示程度高，多用于赞叹，中间的形容词或心理动词大多是褒义词。例如：

In the other case, the degree is so high that the speaker uses it for praise. The central component is always a commendatory term. For example:

5. 我们的朋友太好了！
6. 今天的早饭太好了！
7. 认识你们我太高兴了！

※ 练习：请用感叹句"太……了"回答问题 Please answer the questions with exclamatory sentence "太……了"

1. 五点起床早吗？
   _____。

2. 明天天气好吗？
   _____。

3. 明天没有课，你高兴吗？
   _____。

4. 明天我们早上七点到教室，好吗？
   _____。

综合练习 Comprehensive Exercises

一、根据汉字写拼音 Write Pinyin according to Chinese characters

1. 现在_____   3. 教室_____   5. 星期_____

2. 起床_____   4. 睡觉_____   6. 明天_____

二、朗读语句 Read aloud

1. 星期一
2. 星期天
3. 差一刻九点

4. 现在几点？
5. 今天星期几？
6. 明天没有课，太好了！

三、替换练习 Substitution drills

1. 现在 <u>差一刻十二点</u>。

> 早上八点一刻
> 中午十二点
> 差一刻三点

2. 明天 <u>星期几</u>？

> 星期一
> 星期五
> 星期六

3. 太好了!

> 多
> 晚
> 高兴

四、选词填空 Use the following words to fill in the blanks

> 就　前　到　刻　差

1. 妈妈早上五点_____起床。

2. 我们上午十点一_____下课。

3. 现在_____五分十二点。

4. 你几点_____教室?

5. 我晚上(wǎnshang, evening)十二点_____睡觉。

五、根据课文内容回答问题 Answer the following questions according to the text

1. 现在几点?

2. 月亮明天几点起床? 几点到教室?

3. 明天有课吗?

4. 明天为什么没有课?

六、根据课文内容填空 Fill in the blanks according to the text

现在_____一刻十二点,月亮说(shuō, to say)太_____了,睡觉吧,明天有课,六点半_____起床,八点_____到教室。美丽说明天没有课。_____没有课? 明天是_____,太_____了!

七、汉字书写 Write Chinese characters

现	王 + 见										
	一	二	干	王	却	玥	现	现			
在	一	ナ	才	左	右	在					
太	一	ナ	大	太							
晚	日 + 免										
	丨	冂	日	日	旷	旷	晘	晗	晚	晚	晚
睡	日 + 垂										
	丨	冂	冂	日	日	旷	旷	盯	眂	睡	睡	睡
明	日 + 月										
	丨	冂	日	日	旫	明	明	明			

语言任务 Language Tasks

一、阅读理解 Reading comprehension

李真今天早上八点上课，中午十一点四十分下课，下午也有课。王晨今天没有课，他下午读书，写作业，玩儿电脑游戏。明天是星期六，他们都没有课。

读后判断 True or false

1. 李真今天下午没有课。　　　　　　　　　　　　　　　　（　）

2. 今天是星期五。　　　　　　　　　　　　　　　　　　　（　）

3. 明天王晨和李真都没有课。　　　　　　　　　　　　　　（　）

二、口头表达 Oral expression

任务名称：今天你做什么？

Task: What do you do today?

任务要求：1. 三名学生一组，互相询问今天的安排。

2. 三名学生一起完成表格。

Requirements: 1. Work in groups of three and ask each other about their plans today.

2. Work in groups of three and complete the table together.

Reference words: 早上　中午　下午　星期六　上课　下课　读书　写作业　玩儿电脑游戏　做什么

名字	早上	中午	下午

第八课
Lesson 8

Píngguǒ duōshao qián yì jīn?
苹果 多少 钱 一斤?
How much is a *jin* of apples?

学习目标 Learning Objectives

1. Language Function: Ask about and express the price of goods.
2. Language Points: Mental verb "想"; Expressions for money; Adverb "还" (1); Modal verb "可以" (1).

热身活动 Warming-up

1. 来中国以后，你常常在哪儿买东西？
   Where do you usually shop in China?

2. 你用过中国的哪些购物网站？
   What Chinese shopping websites have you ever used?

课文（一）
Text（Ⅰ）

(Jin Long is shopping in a shop.)

shòuhuòyuán: Nín xiǎng mǎi shénme?
售货员： 您 想 买 什么？

Jīn Lóng: Wǒ xiǎng mǎi shuǐguǒ. Píngguǒ duōshao qián yì jīn?
金龙： 我 想 买 水果。苹果 多少 钱一斤？

shòuhuòyuán: Sì kuài qián yì jīn.
售货员： 四块 钱一斤。

Jīn Lóng: Shí kuài qián yì jīn, tài guì le!
金龙： 十块 钱一斤，太贵了！

shòuhuòyuán: Bú shì shí kuài, shì sì kuài, yī-èr-sān-sì de "sì".
售货员： 不是十块，是四块，一二三 四 的"四"。

Jīn Lóng: Duìbuqǐ, wǒ shì liúxuéshēng, Hànyǔ bú tài hǎo.
金龙： 对不起，我是 留学生，汉语 不太好。

shòuhuòyuán: Méi guānxi. Nín mǎi jǐ jīn?
售货员： 没 关系。您 买 几斤？

Jīn Lóng: Sì jīn, yī-èr-sān-sì de "sì".
金龙： 四斤，一二 三 四 的"四"。

Shop assistant: What do you want to buy?
Jin Long: I want to buy fruit. How much is a *jin* of apples?
Shop assistant: Four *yuan* a *jin*.
Jin Long: Ten *yuan* a *jin*?! That's too expensive!
Shop assistant: No, it's not ten *yuan*. It's four *yuan*—one, two, three, four—four.
Jin Long: Sorry. I'm an international student. My Chinese isn't good.
Shop assistant: It's fine. How many do you want to buy?
Jin Long: Four *jin*—one, two, three, four—four.

第八课　苹果多少钱一斤？
Lesson 8　How much is a *jin* of apples?

生词 New words

1. 售货员	shòuhuòyuán	n.	shop assistant
2. 想	xiǎng	v.	to want to, to would like to
3. 买	mǎi	v.	to buy
4. 水果	shuǐguǒ	n.	fruit
5. 苹果	píngguǒ	n.	apple
6. 钱	qián	n.	money
7. 斤	jīn	m.	*jin*, a unit of weight, equivalent to 500g
8. 块	kuài	m.	*yuan*, the basic currency unit in China
9. 贵	guì	adj.	expensive

专名 Proper nouns

汉语	Hànyǔ	Chinese

语言点 Language Points

一、心理动词"想" Mental verb "想"

心理动词"想"常用在一般动词前面表示愿望或者打算。这时,"想"的前面可以出现程度副词"很""非常"以及否定副词"不"等。例如:

The mental verb "想" is often used in front of general verbs to express wishes or plans. In this case, the adverbs of degree "很", "非常" and the negative adverb "不", etc. can be added in front of "想". For example:

1. 我想买水果。
2. 马大为想买书。
3. 我非常想吃苹果。
4. 他今天不想吃水果。

※ 练习：请用心理动词"想"回答问题　Please answer the questions with mental verb "想".

1. 今天你想吃什么？
   _____。

2. 明天你想几点起床？
   _____。

3. 过生日的时候，你想和谁一起吃饭？
   _____。

4. 今天你想几点睡觉？
   _____。

二、钱数表达法　Expressions for money

中国的货币有三个常用单位——"元（yuán）""角（jiǎo）""分（fēn）"，口语中我们一般用"块（kuài）""毛（máo）""分"。例如：

There are three commonly used units of currency in China: "元 (yuán)", "角 (jiǎo)", and "分 (fēn)". In colloquial language, "块 (kuài)", "毛 (máo)" and "分" are generally used. For example:

¥5.00　　　五元/五块

¥0.5　　　五角/五毛

¥0.05　　　五分

在口语中，当"块"是唯一的货币单位，而前面的数字不是单音节时，"块"可以省略。例如：

In spoken language, when "块" is the only monetary unit and the preceding number is not a single syllable, "块" can be omitted. For example:

¥16.00　　　十六（块）

¥108.00　　　一百零八（块）

在口语中，当"角/毛""分"是最后且不是唯一的货币单位时，"角/毛""分"可以省略。例如：

第八课　苹果多少钱一斤？
Lesson 8　How much is a *jin* of apples?

In spoken language, when "角/毛" and "分" are the last and not the only monetary unit, "角/毛" and "分" can be omitted. For example:

¥7.99　　　　七块九毛九（分）

¥11.20　　　 十一块二

¥365.40　　　三百六十五块四（毛）

¥1080.02　　 一千零八十块零二（分）

当询问某物价格时，汉语常用"N + 多少钱 + 一 + M？"或者"一 + M + N + 多少钱？"等句式。例如：

When asking about the price of something, "N + 多少钱 + 一 + M？" or "一 + M + N + 多少钱？" is often used in Chinese. For example:

1. A：苹果多少钱一斤？

　 B：五块五一斤。

2. A：一斤苹果多少钱？

　 B：五块五。

※ 练习：请用汉字写出下列价格　Please write down the following prices in Chinese

1. ¥2.50

　_____

2. ¥299

　_____

3. ¥10

　_____

4. ¥364.78

　_____

综合练习 Comprehensive Exercises

一、根据汉字写拼音 Write Pinyin according to Chinese characters

1. 苹果_____ 3. 块_____ 5. 买_____

2. 钱_____ 4. 汉语_____ 6. 斤_____

二、朗读语句 Read aloud

1. 吃苹果
2. 买水果
3. 买三斤水果

4. 你喜欢吃什么水果？
5. 我喜欢吃苹果。
6. 一斤苹果三块五。

三、替换练习 Substitution drills

1. 我想 买水果。

   吃苹果
   写作业
   玩儿游戏

2. 苹果 多少钱一 斤？

   西瓜（xīguā, watermelon）
   香蕉（xiāngjiāo, banana）
   橙子（chéngzi, orange）

   个
   斤
   斤

第八课　苹果多少钱一斤？
Lesson 8　How much is a *jin* of apples?

3. 不是 十块，是 四块。

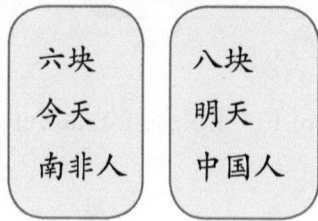

四、选词填空 Use the following words to fill in the blanks

买　想　块　水果　汉语

1. 你_____几斤苹果？

2. 一斤苹果几_____钱？

3. 那些_____多少钱？

4. 我今天不_____上课。

5. 我非常喜欢学_____。

五、根据课文内容回答问题 Answer the following questions according to the text

1. 金龙想买什么？

2. 苹果多少钱一斤？

3. 金龙想买几斤苹果？

六、根据课文内容填空 Fill in the blanks according to the text

金龙_____买苹果，苹果一斤四块钱，金龙说（shuō, to say）十块钱一斤太_____了。售货员说_____十块，_____四块，一二三四的"四"。金龙说他是留学生，汉语_____。他_____买四斤苹果，不是十斤，是四斤。

七、汉字书写　Write Chinese characters

买	一	𠃍	𠃌	𰀁	买	买					
水	亅	刂	水	水							
果	丶	冂	日	曰	旦	甲	男	果			
钱	钅+戋										
	丿	𠂉	𠂉	𠂊	钅	钅	钅	钱	钱	钱	
块	土+夬										
	一	十	土	扌	圠	块	块				
汉	氵+又										
	丶	冫	氵	汈	汉						

第八课　苹果多少钱一斤？

Lesson 8　How much is a *jin* of apples?

课文（二）
Text（Ⅱ）

(Ma Dawei is shopping in a shop.)

Mǎ Dàwéi: Nǐ hǎo, yì píng shuǐ duōshao qián?
马大为：你好，一瓶 水 多少 钱？

shòuhuòyuán: Liǎng kuài wǔ.
售货员：两 块 五。

Mǎ Dàwéi: Wǒ yào liǎng píng.
马大为：我 要 两 瓶。

shòuhuòyuán: Hái yào biéde ma?
售货员：还 要 别的 吗？

Mǎ Dàwéi: Hái yào yí gè miànbāo. Yígòng duōshao qián?
马大为：还要一个 面包。一共 多少 钱？

shòuhuòyuán: Yígòng shí kuài sān máo qián.
售货员：一共 十 块 三 毛 钱。

Mǎ Dàwéi: Kěyǐ shǒujī zhīfù ma?
马大为：可以手机支付吗？

shòuhuòyuán: Dāngrán kěyǐ.
售货员：当然 可以。

Mǎ Dàwéi: Xièxie.
马大为：谢谢。

shòuhuòyuán: Bú kèqi.
售货员：不客气。

Ma Dawei: Hello, how much is a bottle of water?
Shop assistant: Two *yuan* and five *mao*.
Ma Dawei: I'd like to buy two bottles.
Shop assistant: Anything else?
Ma Dawei: I also want a bread. How much in total?
Shop assistant: Ten *yuan* and three *mao* in total.
Ma Dawei: Can I pay by my phone?
Shop assistant: Of course.
Ma Dawei: Thank you.
Shop assistant: You are welcome.

生词 New words

1.	瓶	píng	m./n.	a bottle of; bottle
2.	水	shuǐ	n.	water
3.	要	yào	v.	to want, to ask for
4.	还	hái	adv.	in addition, also, still
5.	别的	biéde	pron.	other
6.	面包	miànbāo	n.	bread
7.	一共	yígòng	adv.	altogether, in total
8.	毛	máo	m.	mao, a fractional unit of money in China, ten cents
9.	可以	kěyǐ	mod.v.	may, can
10.	支付	zhīfù	v.	to pay
11.	当然	dāngrán	adv.	of course, certainly
12.	谢谢	xièxie	v.	to thank
13.	不客气	bú kèqi		you are welcome

语言点 Language Points

一、副词"还"（1） Adverb "还" (1)

副词"还"用在动词前面，可以表示对前面的内容进行补充。例如：

The adverb "还" is used in front of verbs to supplement the previous content. For example:

1. 我要两瓶水，还要一个面包。

2. 我买书，还买水果。

3. 明天我想去买书，还想和朋友一起吃饭。

※ 练习：请用副词"还"回答问题 Please answer the questions with adverb "还"

1. 你有哪些外国朋友？

_____。

2. 你想买什么?

　　_____。

3. 你想吃什么?

　　_____。

4. 你要什么?

　　_____。

5. 你认识谁?

　　_____。

6. 你想家吗?

　　_____。

二、能愿动词"可以"（1） Modal verb "可以" (1)

能愿动词"可以"用在动词或动词短语前面，表示能够。例如：

The modal verb "可以" is used in front of a verb or verbal phrase, which means to be able to. For example:

1. 可以手机支付吗?

2. 一百块钱可以买很多苹果。

3. 明天没有课，我们可以和朋友一起吃饭。

※ 练习：组词成句 Group words into sentences

1. 下午　玩儿电脑游戏　可以　我们

　　_____。

2. 五瓶水　买　可以　十块钱

　　_____。

3. 和朋友玩儿　星期六　可以　我们

　　_____。

综合练习 Comprehensive Exercises

一、根据汉字写拼音 Write Pinyin according to Chinese characters

1. 可以_____
2. 谢谢_____
3. 一共_____
4. 当然_____
5. 别的_____
6. 面包_____

二、朗读语句 Read aloud

1. 一斤苹果
2. 两瓶水
3. 三个面包

4. 我要一斤苹果，还要一瓶水。
5. 他想买一瓶水。
6. 一共三十五块钱。

三、替换练习 Substitution drills

1. <u>一瓶水</u> 多少钱？

　　一斤苹果
　　一个手机
　　一个面包

2. 还要 <u>别的</u> 吗？

　　面包
　　苹果
　　水

第八课　苹果多少钱一斤？
Lesson 8　How much is a *jin* of apples?

3. 可以 <u>手机支付</u> 吗？

> 一起吃饭
> 现在下课
> 玩儿游戏

四、选词填空 Use the following words to fill in the blanks

> 一共　可以　当然　还　瓶

1. 这些书_____多少钱？

2. _____手机支付吗？

3. 一_____水多少钱？

4. 我_____认识他，他是我的好朋友。

5. 我要一瓶水，_____要一个面包。

五、根据课文内容回答问题 Answer the following questions according to the text

1. 马大为想买什么？

2. 一瓶水多少钱？

3. 马大为还要别的吗？

4. 两瓶水和一个面包一共多少钱？

六、根据课文内容填空 Fill in the blanks according to the text

一瓶水_____，马大为想买_____水，还想买一_____面包。_____十块三_____钱，_____手机_____。

七、汉字书写 Write Chinese characters

要	西+女											
	一	一	一	西	西	西	要	要	要			
还	辶+不											
	一	ア	不	不	不	还	还					
共	一	十	丗	丗	共	共						
可	丁+口											
	一	一	一	可	可							
以	Ｖ	Ｖ	以	以								
谢	讠+射											
	、	讠	讠	讠	讠	讠	讠	讱	谢	谢	谢	

语言任务 Language Tasks

一、阅读理解 Reading comprehension

一斤苹果四块钱，金龙想买两斤。他还要两瓶水和一个面包。两瓶水一共五块钱，一个面包六块五。这些一共多少钱？

读后判断 True or false

1. 两斤苹果一共六块钱。 （ ）
2. 一瓶水五块钱。 （ ）
3. 苹果、水和面包一共十六块五。 （ ）

二、口头表达 Oral expression

任务名称：一共多少钱？
Task: How much is it?

第八课　苹果多少钱一斤？
Lesson 8　How much is a *jin* of apples?

任务要求：两名学生一组，一名是售货员，一名是买东西的顾客，二人互相询问和介绍价格。

Requirements: Work in pairs. One acts as a shop assistant, and the other acts as a consumer. Ask about and introduce the price.

Reference words: 苹果　一斤　水　瓶　面包　一共　别的　要　买　多少钱

第九课 Lesson 9

Wǒ gēge zài yīyuàn gōngzuò
我哥哥在医院 工作
My elder brother works in a hospital

学习目标 Learning Objectives

1. Language Function: Ask about or describe the job.
2. Language Points: Verb "在" and preposition "在"; Modal particle "吧" (2); Adverb "最"; Interrogative pronoun "哪儿"; Adverb "一直".

热身活动 Warming-up

1. 下面这些人，你觉得谁的工作最忙？谁的工作最轻松？
   Who is the busiest and who is the most relaxed?

2. 下面这些地方，你最喜欢去哪儿？最不喜欢去哪儿？
   Where do you want to go the most? Where do you want to go the least?

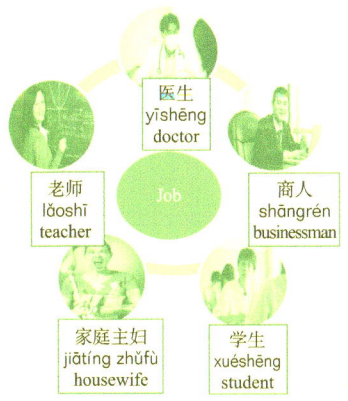

117

课文（一）
Text (I)

(Meili and Wang Chen are chatting on campus.)

Měilì: Nǐ gēge yě shì xuésheng ma?
美丽：你哥哥也是学生吗？

Wáng Chén: Bù, tā shì yīshēng, zài yīyuàn gōngzuò.
王晨：不，他是医生，在医院工作。

Měilì: Tā hěn máng ba?
美丽：他很忙吧？

Wáng Chén: Duì, fēicháng máng.
王晨：对，非常忙。

Měilì: Zài nǐmen jiā, tā zuì máng ba?
美丽：在你们家，他最忙吧？

Wáng Chén: Bù, zài wǒmen jiā, māma zuì máng.
王晨：不，在我们家，妈妈最忙。

Měilì: Tā zài nǎr gōngzuò?
美丽：她在哪儿工作？

Wáng Chén: Tā zài jiā, tā shì jiātíng zhǔfù. Tā méiyǒu xiūxi shíjiān.
王晨：她在家，她是家庭主妇。她没有休息时间。

Meili: Is your elder brother also a student?
Wang Chen: No, he is a doctor. He works in a hospital.
Meili: He is very busy, isn't he?
Wang Chen: Yes, he is.
Meili: Is he the busiest person in your family?
Wang Chen: No, in my family, mom is the busiest one.
Meili: Where does she work?
Wang Chen: She is at home, and she is a housewife. She has no time to rest.

生词 New words

1. 哥哥	gēge	n.	elder brother
2. 医生	yīshēng	n.	doctor

3. 在	zài	*prep./v.*	in, at; to stay
4. 医院	yīyuàn	*n.*	hospital
5. 工作	gōngzuò	*v./n.*	to work; job
6. 忙	máng	*adj.*	busy
7. 最	zuì	*adv.*	most
8. 哪儿	nǎr	*pron.*	where
9. 家庭	jiātíng	*n.*	family
10. 主妇	zhǔfù	*n.*	housewife
11. 休息	xiūxi	*v.*	to rest
12. 时间	shíjiān	*n.*	time

语言点 Language Points

一、动词"在"与介词"在"　Verb "在" and preposition "在"

动词"在"表示人或事物所处的地点。例如：

The verb "在" means the place where a person or thing is. For example:

1. 妈妈在家。

2. 美丽在教室。

3. 哥哥在医院。

介词"在"常与名词、代词等组成介词短语做状语，用在动词或动词短语前，表示动作行为发生的地点或时间。例如：

The preposition "在" forms an adverbial modifier with nouns, pronouns, etc., and is used before a verb or a verbal phrase to indicate the place or time of the action. For example:

4. 妈妈在家休息。

5. 哥哥在医院工作。

6. 金龙在七月过生日。

※ 练习：请用"在"回答问题 Please answer the questions with "在"

1. 你在哪儿？

   _____。

2. 王晨在哪儿学习？

   _____。

3. 王晨的哥哥在哪儿工作？

   _____。

二、语气助词"吧"（2） Modal particle "吧" (2)

语气助词"吧"可以用于对不确定的情况进行询问。例如：

The modal particle "吧" can be used to inquire about uncertain situations. For example:

1. 你哥哥是医生，他很忙吧？
2. 可以手机支付吧？
3. 明天星期一，你们有课吧？

※ 练习：请用语气助词"吧"完成对话 Please complete the dialogues with modal particle "吧"

1. A：_____？

   B：对，我妈妈很忙。

2. A：_____？

   B：对，我下午没有课。

3. A：_____？

   B：对，我是留学生。

4. A：_____？

   B：不是，他是我哥哥。

三、副词"最"　　Adverb "最"

副词"最"常用在形容词或心理动词前,表示在一定范围内程度最高。例如:

The adverb "最" is often used before adjectives or mental verbs, indicating the highest degree within a certain range. For example:

1. 在我们家,妈妈最忙。
2. 在我们学院,王晨学习最好。
3. 美丽是我最好的朋友。
4. 月亮很想家,她最想她的妈妈。

※ 练习:请用副词"最"回答问题 Please answer the questions with adverb "最"

1. 你最好的朋友是谁?
   _____。

2. 在你们班(bān, class),谁的汉语最好?
   _____。

3. 在你们家,谁最忙?
   _____。

4. 今天早上,谁最早到教室?
   _____。

四、疑问代词"哪儿"　　Interrogative pronoun "哪儿"

疑问代词"哪儿"可以用来询问地点。有疑问代词的问句,其语序与陈述句相同。例如:

The interrogative pronoun "哪儿" can be used to ask about a place. Questions with interrogative pronouns have the same word order with declarative sentences. For example:

1. 马大为在哪儿?
2. 李真在哪儿上课?
3. 你到哪儿买面包?

※ 练习：请用疑问代词"哪儿"完成对话 Please complete the dialogues with intorrogative pronoun "哪儿"

1. A：_____？
   B：我在教室。

2. A：_____？
   B：妈妈在家里。

3. A：_____？
   B：哥哥在医院工作。

4. A：_____？
   B：我在家吃早饭。

综合练习 Comprehensive Exercises

一、根据汉字写拼音 Write Pinyin according to Chinese characters

1. 哥哥_____   3. 工作_____   5. 休息_____
2. 医院_____   4. 医生_____   6. 时间_____

二、朗读语句 Read aloud

1. 在家
2. 在医院
3. 在教室

4. 你在哪儿工作？
5. 我在医院工作。
6. 妈妈工作非常忙。

三、替换练习 Substitution drills

1. <u>王晨的哥哥</u> 在 <u>医院</u> 工作。

王晨的妈妈	家
李真的朋友	学校
李真的妈妈	医学院

2. 你哥哥也是 学生 吗?

> 医生
> 老师
> 护士

3. 他是医生，他很 忙 吧?

> 今天是他的生日
> 金龙在中国没有朋友
> 今天没有休息

> 高兴
> 想家
> 累（lèi, tired）

四、选词填空 Use the following words to fill in the blanks

> 休息　最　忙　时间　在

1. 王晨的哥哥是医生，他非常_____。

2. 他爸爸是老师，_____学校（xuéxiào, school）工作。

3. 我们今天_____，不上课。

4. 你明天早上有_____吗?

5. 过生日的时候，我_____想家。

五、根据课文内容回答问题 Answer the following questions according to the text

1. 王晨的哥哥也是学生吗?

2. 王晨的哥哥很忙吧?

3. 在王晨家，谁最忙?

4. 王晨的妈妈在哪儿工作?

六、根据课文内容填空 Fill in the blanks according to the text

王晨的哥哥不是学生，是医生，在医院_____，很_____。他哥哥不是家里最忙的人。在他家，妈妈_____忙。妈妈是_____，没有_____时间。

七、汉字书写 Write Chinese characters

哥	可+可	一	丆	〒	可	可	могут 亘	픔	哥	哥			
医	匚+矢	一	丆	厅	三	至	矢	医					
作	亻+乍	丿	亻	仁	仵	竹	作	作					
忙	忄+亡	丶	丶	忄	忙	忙	忙						
最	曰+取	丨	冂	冃	曰	旦	早	昌	昌	昌	最	最	
时	日+寸	丨	冂	日	日	日一	时	时					

课文（二）
Text (Ⅱ)

(Wang Chen is calling Jin Long.)

Jīn Lóng: Wèi, Wáng Chén.
金龙：喂，王晨。

Wáng Chén: Jīn Lóng, wǎnshang wǒmen qù kàn diànyǐng ba.
王晨：金龙，晚上我们去看电影吧。

Jīn Lóng: Tài hǎo le, wǒ zuì xǐhuan kàn diànyǐng.
金龙：太好了，我最喜欢看电影。

Wáng Chén: Mǎ Dàwéi yě xǐhuan kàn diànyǐng, tā qù ma?
王晨：马大为也喜欢看电影，他去吗？

Jīn Lóng: Tā bú qù.
金龙：他不去。

Wáng Chén: Wèi shénme?
王晨：为什么？

Jīn Lóng: Zuótiān wǎnshang tā yìzhí zài fángjiān kàn diànyǐng, jīntiān shàngwǔ tā shuō yǎnjing hěn téng.
金龙：昨天晚上他一直在房间看电影，今天上午他说眼睛很疼。

Wáng Chén: Tā xiànzài zài nǎr?
王晨：他现在在哪儿？

Jīn Lóng: Tā zài yīyuàn kàn yǎnjing.
金龙：他在医院看眼睛。

Jin Long: Hello, Wang Chen!
Wang Chen: Jin Long, shall we watch a movie tonight?
Jin Long: Great! Movies are my favorite.
Wang Chen: Ma Dawei likes watching movies as well. Is he going, too?
Jin Long: No, he isn't.
Wang Chen: Why?
Jin Long: He watched movies last night in his room, so this morning his eyes hurt.
Wang Chen: Where is he?
Jin Long: He is seeing an ophthalmologist in the hospital.

第九课　我哥哥在医院工作
Lesson 9　My elder brother works in a hospital

生词 New words

1.	喂	wèi	int.	hello
2.	晚上	wǎnshang	n.	evening
3.	去	qù	v.	to go
4.	看电影	kàn diànyǐng	VO	to see a movie
	看	kàn	v.	to see, to watch, to treat (a patient or an illness)
	电影	diànyǐng	n.	movie
5.	昨天	zuótiān	n.	yesterday
6.	一直	yìzhí	adv.	continuously, always
7.	房间	fángjiān	n.	room
8.	上午	shàngwǔ	n.	morning
9.	说	shuō	v.	to say
10.	眼睛	yǎnjing	n.	eye
11.	疼	téng	adj.	painful, aching

语言点 Language Points

副词"一直"（1） Adverb "一直" (1)

副词"一直"常用在动词性短语或形容词性短语前，表示动作或者状态持续不变。例如：

The adverb "一直" is often used before verbal phrases or adjectival phrases to indicate that an action or state remains unchanged. For example:

1. 昨天晚上他一直在房间看电影。
2. 今天我一直在家。
3. 哥哥昨天一直在医院工作。
4. 哥哥工作一直很忙。

※ 练习：请用副词"一直"回答问题 Please answer the questions with adverb "一直"

1. 你下午在哪儿？
   _____。

2. 苹果贵吗？
   _____。

3. 妈妈工作忙吗？
   _____。

4. 你想家吗？
   _____。

综合练习 Comprehensive Exercises

一、根据汉字写拼音 Write Pinyin according to Chinese characters

1. 电影_____   3. 昨天_____   5. 眼睛_____

2. 晚上_____   4. 上午_____   6. 房间_____

二、朗读语句 Read aloud

1. 看电影
2. 写作业
3. 读书

4. 我们去看电影吧。
5. 我的眼睛一直很疼。
6. 我不想看电影。

三、替换练习 Substitution drills

1. 晚上我们去 <u>看电影</u> 吧。

   吃饭
   哥哥家
   买水果

第九课　我哥哥在医院工作
Lesson 9　My elder brother works in a hospital

2. 他一直 在房间 看电影。

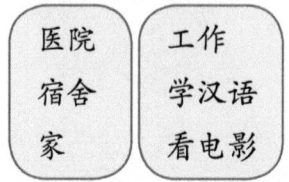

3. 他在 医院 看眼睛。

医院	工作
宿舍	学汉语
家	看电影

四、选词填空 Use the following words to fill in the blanks

去 看 说 一直 疼

1. 金龙想和王晨_____泰国玩儿。

2. 今天晚上我们一起_____电影吧。

3. 我上午_____在房间看书。

4. 他_____下午可以去学校（xuéxiào，school）。

5. 你的眼睛_____吗?

五、根据课文内容回答问题 Answer the following questions according to the text

1. 王晨晚上想做什么?

2. 金龙最喜欢什么?

3. 马大为晚上去看电影吗?

4. 马大为为什么不去看电影?

六、根据课文内容填空 Fill in the blanks according to the text

王晨晚上想和金龙_____看电影，金龙很高兴，他很_____看电影。马大为也很喜欢看电影，他今天不去，他现在_____看眼睛。昨天晚上马大为_____在房间看电影，今天上午他_____眼睛非常_____。

七、汉字书写 Write Chinese characters

去	一	十	土	去	去			
看	手+目							
	一	二	三	手	看	看	看	看
昨	日+乍							
	丨	冂	日	日	旷	旷	昨	昨
房	户+方							
	丶	一	彐	户	户	房	房	
说	讠+兑							
	丶	讠	讠	讠	讱	说	说	说
疼	疒+冬							
	丶	一	广	广	疒	疒	疼	疼	疼

语言任务 Language Tasks

一、阅读理解 Reading comprehension

王晨家有四口人，他的哥哥和爸爸在医院工作，他们工作都非常忙。在他家，哥哥和爸爸不是最忙的人，最忙的人是妈妈。妈妈是家庭主妇，没有休息时间，每天（měi tiān, every day）都很忙，也很累（lèi, tired）。

第九课　我哥哥在医院工作
Lesson 9　My elder brother works in a hospital

读后判断 True or false

1. 王晨的爸爸不工作。( )
2. 王晨的妈妈是护士。( )
3. 王晨的爸爸和哥哥都是医生。( )

二、口头表达 Oral expression

任务名称：你家人做什么工作？

Task: What does your family do?

任务要求：两名学生一组，互相询问家人的职业，必要时可用英语。

Requirements: Work in pairs and ask each other about the occupations of their family members. You may use English when necessary.

Reference words: 在　工作　医院　忙　家庭主妇　休息　时间

第十课 Lesson 10

Lái wǒ jiā wánr ba!
来我家玩儿吧!
Come round to my home!

学习目标 Learning Objectives

1. Language Function: Describe or introduce living conditions.
2. Language Points: Interrogative pronoun "怎么样"; Modal particle "呢" (2); Gearing sentence; Verb "离".

热身活动 Warming-up

1. 来中国以前,你住在哪儿?(宿舍、小区、公寓)来中国以后呢?
   Where did you live before you come to China? (dormitory, community, apartment) Where are you living now?

2. 你觉得现在住的地方怎么样?
   How do you like your current living condition?

131

课文（一）
Text (I)

(Li Zhen and Meili are chatting in a café.)

Lǐ Zhēn: Nǐ zhù zài xuéxiào de liúxuéshēng sùshè ma?
李真：你住在学校的留学生宿舍吗？

Měilì: Duì.
美丽：对。

Lǐ Zhēn: Liúxuéshēng sùshè zěnmeyàng?
李真：留学生宿舍怎么样？

Měilì: Hěn hǎo, yě hěn fāngbiàn.
美丽：很好，也很方便。

Lǐ Zhēn: Sùshè lǐbian yǒu shénme?
李真：宿舍里边有什么？

Měilì: Zhuōzi, yǐzi, chuáng hé diànshì.
美丽：桌子、椅子、床和电视。

Lǐ Zhēn: Měi gè sùshè yǒu jǐ gè rén?
李真：每个宿舍有几个人？

Měilì: Liǎng gè rén. Nǐ zhù zài nǎr ne?
美丽：两个人。你住在哪儿呢？

Lǐ Zhēn: Wǒ zhù zài jiā li.
李真：我住在家里。

Měilì: Nǐ zhēn xìngfú!
美丽：你真幸福！

Li Zhen: Do you live in the internatial students' dorm of school?
Meili: Yes.
Li Zhen: How about the international students' dormitory?
Meili: Very good and also very convenient.
Li Zhen: What are there in the dormitory?
Meili: A table, a chair, a bed and a TV set.
Li Zhen: How many people are there in each dorm?
Meili: Two. Where do you live?
Li Zhen: I live at home.
Meili: You are so happy!

生词 New words

1.	住	zhù	v.	to live, to reside
2.	学校	xuéxiào	n.	school
3.	怎么样	zěnmeyàng	pron.	how about
4.	方便	fāngbiàn	adj.	convenient
5.	里边	lǐbian	n.	inside, within, in
	里	lǐ	n.	inside
6.	桌子	zhuōzi	n.	table
7.	椅子	yǐzi	n.	chair
8.	床	chuáng	n.	bed
9.	电视	diànshì	n.	television
10.	每个	měi gè		each of
	每	měi	pron.	each, every
11.	幸福	xìngfú	adj.	happy

语言点 Language Points

一、疑问代词"怎么样"　　Interrogative pronoun "怎么样"

疑问代词"怎么样"用来询问人或事物的性质状态，一般用在句尾。例如：

The interrogative pronoun "怎么样" is used to inquire about the nature of a person or thing, and is generally used at the end of a sentence. For example:

1. 留学生宿舍怎么样？
2. 这个手机怎么样？
3. 你哥哥工作怎么样？
4. 明天天气怎么样？

※ 练习：回答问题 Answer the questions

1. 你的宿舍怎么样？

　　_____。

第十课　来我家玩儿吧！
Lesson 10　Come round to my home!

2. 你的手机怎么样?

　　_____。

3. 你的汉语怎么样?

　　_____。

4. 你的同学怎么样?

　　_____。

二、语气助词"呢"（2）　　Modal particle "呢" (2)

语气助词"呢"用在疑问句的末尾，有加强疑问语气的作用。例如：

The modal particle "呢" is used at the end of interrogative sentences to strengthen the interrogative mood. For example:

1. 你住在哪儿呢?

2. 他叫什么名字呢?

3. 一个面包多少钱呢?

※ 练习：请用语气助词"呢"完成对话　Please complete the dialogues with modal particle "呢"

1. A：_____?

　　B：我在教室里上课。

2. A：_____?

　　B：他是中国人。

3. A：_____?

　　B：苹果六块钱一斤。

4. A：_____?

　　B：我们的宿舍很好。

综合练习 Comprehensive Exercises

一、根据汉字写拼音 Write Pinyin according to Chinese characters

1. 学校＿＿＿＿
2. 方便＿＿＿＿
3. 桌子＿＿＿＿
4. 椅子＿＿＿＿
5. 电视＿＿＿＿
6. 里边＿＿＿＿

二、朗读语句 Read aloud

1. 住在学校
2. 住在家里
3. 住在北京（Běijīng）
4. 你住在哪儿？
5. 我住在学校宿舍。
6. 我住在中国北京。

三、替换练习 Substitution drills

1. 你住在 <u>留学生宿舍</u> 吗？

   家里
   北京
   学校

2. <u>留学生宿舍</u> 怎么样？

   你们的学校
   你哥哥的工作
   你的汉语

3. 每个 <u>宿舍</u> 有几个人？

   房间
   家庭
   教室

第十课　来我家玩儿吧！
Lesson 10　Come round to my home!

四、选词填空 Use the following words to fill in the blanks

> 住　怎么样　里边　每　方便

1. 你的房间_____?
2. 你们_____在学校宿舍吗?
3. 一个人住很_____。
4. _____个手机都很贵。
5. 房间_____有很多人。

五、根据课文内容回答问题 Answer the following questions according to the text

1. 美丽住在哪儿?
2. 留学生宿舍怎么样?
3. 宿舍里边有什么?
4. 每个宿舍有几个人?
5. 李真住在哪儿?

六、根据课文内容填空 Fill in the blanks according to the text

美丽_____留学生宿舍,她说宿舍很好,也很_____。宿舍里边有_____、椅子、_____和电视,_____个宿舍住_____个人。李真不住在_____里,她住在_____里,真_____!

七、汉字书写 Write Chinese characters

| 住 | 亻+主　ノ　亻　亻　仁　住　住 |

校	木+交 一 十 才 木 术 栌 栌 栌 校 校											
方	、 一 亠 方											
里	丨 冂 曱 曰 甲 甲 里											
桌	占+木 丿 卜 上 占 占 卓 卓 桌 桌											
每	𠂉+母 丿 𠂉 𠂉 仁 每 每 每											

第十课　来我家玩儿吧!

Lesson 10　Come round to my home!

课文（二）
Text（Ⅱ）

(Li Zhen is calling Meili.)

Lǐ Zhēn: Měilì, xīngqīliù nǐ yǒu shíjiān ma?
李真：美丽，星期六你有时间吗？

Měilì: Yǒu shíjiān.
美丽：有时间。

Lǐ Zhēn: Lái wǒ jiā wánr ba!
李真：来我家玩儿吧！

Měilì: Hǎo a, nǐ zhù nǎr? Yuǎn ma?
美丽：好啊，你住哪儿？远吗？

Lǐ Zhēn: Xìngfú Xiǎoqū, lí xuéxiào hěn jìn, zuò gōnggòng qìchē shí fēnzhōng.
李真：幸福小区，离学校很近，坐公共汽车十分钟。

Měilì: Zuò jǐ lù gōnggòng qìchē?
美丽：坐几路公共汽车？

Lǐ Zhēn: Zài xuéxiào nánmén zuò 70 lù, zuò liǎng zhàn, dào Xìngfú Xiǎoqū.
李真：在学校南门坐70路，坐两站，到幸福小区。

Měilì: Hǎo, xīngqīliù jiàn!
美丽：好，星期六见！

Li Zhen: Meili, do you have time this Saturday?

Meili: Yes, I do.

Li Zhen: Would you like to come to my home?

Meili: OK. Where do you live? Is it far?

Li Zhen: I live in the Happiness Community, which is very close to the school. It takes you 10 minutes by bus.

Meili: What bus should I take?

Li Zhen: You should take No. 70 bus for two stops and get off at the Happiness Community.

Meili: OK. See you Saturday!

生词 New words

1. 来	lái	*v.*	to come
2. 远	yuǎn	*adj.*	far

3. 小区	xiǎoqū	n.	community
4. 离	lí	v.	to be away from
5. 近	jìn	adj.	near
6. 坐	zuò	v.	to take
7. 公共汽车	gōnggòng qìchē		bus
公共	gōnggòng	adj.	public, common
汽车	qìchē	n.	automobile, car
8. 分钟	fēnzhōng	m.	minute
9. 路	lù	n.	route
10. 南门	nánmén	n.	south gate
南	nán	n.	south
门	mén	n.	entrance, gate, door
11. 站	zhàn	n.	station
12. 见	jiàn	v.	to see, to meet

专名 Proper nouns

幸福小区	Xìngfú Xiǎoqū	the Happiness Community

语言点 Language Points

一、连动句 Gearing sentence

汉语中有一类句子，同一个主语后面有两个或两个以上动词或动词性短语做谓语，这类句子叫连动句。连动句中的动词或动词性短语一般是按照动作行为发生的前后顺序出现的。例如：

There is a kind of sentences in Chinese, which has two or more verbs or verbal phrases behind the same subject to act as predicates. Such sentences are gearing sentences. The verbs or verbal phrases in a gearing sentence generally appear in the order in which the actions occur. For example:

1. 来我家玩儿吧!
2. 我们去教室上课吧。
3. 哥哥去医院工作。

※ 练习：组词成句 Group words into sentences

1. 学习　去　教室　李真

　　_____。

2. 马大为　王晨家　去　玩儿

　　_____。

3. 金龙　同学的宿舍　去　看电影

　　_____。

4. 吃早饭　医院　哥哥　去

　　_____。

二、动词"离"　Verb "离"

动词"离"常用来表示空间或时间上的距离。在表示空间距离的时候，"离"常用在"地点1 + 离 + 地点2 + 远/近"结构中。例如：

The verb "离" is often used to express distance in space or time. When expressing spatial distance, "离" is often used in the structure of "location 1 + 离 + location 2 + 远/近". For example:

1. 我家离学校很远。
2. 教室离宿舍很近。

在表示时间距离的时候，"离"常用在"时间点1 + 离 + 时间点2 + 远/近"结构中。例如：

When expressing time distance, "离" is often used in "time point 1 + 离 + time point 2 + 远/近" structure. For example:

3. 妈妈的生日离元旦很远。
4. 我的生日离护士节很近。

※ 练习：组词成句 Group words into sentences

1. 非常近　宿舍　教室　离

　　_____。

2. 幸福小区　学校　不太远　离

　　_____。

3. 离　南非　中国　很远

　　_____。

4. 医院　我家　离　非常远

　　_____。

综合练习 Comprehensive Exercises

一、根据汉字写拼音 Write Pinyin according to Chinese characters

1. 离_____　　3. 分钟_____　　5. 近_____

2. 坐_____　　4. 远_____　　　6. 小区_____

二、朗读语句 Read aloud

1. 离学校很近
2. 坐公共汽车
3. 坐70路公共汽车
4. 我家离学校不远。
5. 坐公共汽车，坐两站，到幸福小区。
6. 在学校南门坐70路公共汽车可以到我家。

三、替换练习 Substitution drills

1. 来我家 玩儿 吧!

> 写作业
> 看电视
> 玩儿游戏

2. 幸福小区，离 学校 很近。

> 宿舍
> 我家
> 留学生宿舍

> 教室
> 医院
> 学院

四、选词填空 Use the following words to fill in the blanks

> 离　坐　路　分钟　见

1. 我家_____学校很近。

2. 我们还有几_____下课?

3. 18_____公共汽车可以到学校吗?

4. 我星期六有时间，我们在哪儿_____?

5. 我可以_____在这里（zhèlǐ, here）吗?

五、根据课文内容回答问题 Answer the following questions according to the text

1. 李真住在哪儿?

2. 李真家离学校远吗?

3. 坐几路公共汽车可以到李真家?

4. 在哪儿坐公共汽车?

六、根据课文内容填空 Fill in the blanks according to the text

李真想请（to invite）美丽去她家玩儿，美丽星期六有_____。李真_____幸福小区，她家_____学校很近，坐公共汽车十_____就到。就在学校_____坐70路，坐两_____，到幸福小区下车。

七、汉字书写 Write Chinese characters

来	一	ㄱ	丆	二	来	来	来					
远	辶+元											
	一	二	テ	元	辽	远	远					
离	亠+内											
	、	亠	卞	文	产	卤	离	离	离	离		
近	辶+斤											
	一	厂	斤	斤	辽	近	近					
坐	从+土											
	丿	人	从	从	丛	丛	坐	坐				
路	足+各											
	丨	口	口	甲	卫	足	足	趵	政	政	路	路

语言任务 Language Tasks

一、阅读理解 Reading comprehension

美丽住在学校的留学生宿舍，她觉得（juéde, to think）住在宿舍很方便。李真住在幸福小区，她家离学校很近。在学校南门坐公共汽车，一共坐两站，十分钟就可以到她家。

读后判断 True or false

1. 美丽和李真都住在学校里边。　　　　　　　　　　　　　（　）

2. 美丽喜欢住在学校宿舍里。　　　　　　　　　　　　　　（　）

3. 坐公共汽车去李真家很方便。　　　　　　　　　　　　　（　）

二、口头表达 Oral expression

任务名称：邀请朋友来家玩儿。

Task: Invite friends home.

任务要求：1. 两名学生一组，一人邀请另一人来家里做客。

　　　　　2. 用所学生词和句子说明如何去家里。

Requirements: 1. Work in pairs. One invites the other to visit his/her house.

　　　　　　 2. Use the new words and sentences to describe how to get there.

Reference words: 来　去　坐　公共汽车　离　远　近　站　路　分钟

第十一课 Lesson 11

Jiěpōulóu zài túshūguǎn de dōngbian
解剖楼 在 图书馆 的 东边
The anatomy building is to the east of the library

学习目标 Learning Objectives

1. Language Function: Ask about and describe the location of someone or something.
2. Language Points: Verb-reduplication "AA" type; Preposition "给"; Select question; Adverb "就"; Noun of locality.

热身活动 Warming-up

1. 这是什么地方?
   What's this place?

2. 你知道学校图书馆在哪儿吗?
   Do you know where the school library is?

课文（一）
Text（Ⅰ）

(Ma Dawei is asking for directions on campus.)

Mǎ Dàwéi: Tóngxué, qǐngwèn jiěpōulóu zài nǎr?
马大为：同学，请问 解剖楼在哪儿？

tóngxué 1: Bù hǎoyìsi, wǒ bù zhīdào. Nǐ qù wènwen biérén ba.
同学1：不好意思，我不知道。你去问问别人吧。

Mǎ Dàwéi: Xièxie.
马大为：谢谢。

(Ma Dawei goes to ask another student.)

Mǎ Dàwéi: Qǐngwèn, jiěpōulóu zài shénme dìfang?
马大为：请问，解剖楼在什么地方？

tóngxué 2: Jiěpōulóu zài túshūguǎn de dōngbian.
同学2：解剖楼在图书馆的东边。

Mǎ Dàwéi: Túshūguǎn zài nǎr?
马大为：图书馆在哪儿？

tóngxué 2: Túshūguǎn zài jiàoxuélóu de hòumiàn.
同学2：图书馆在教学楼的后面。

Mǎ Dàwéi: Xièxie.
马大为：谢谢。

tóngxué 2: Bú kèqi.
同学2：不客气。

Ma Dawei: Excuse me, where is the anatomy building, please?
  Student 1: I am sorry, I don't know. Ask someone else, please.
Ma Dawei: Thank you.

Ma Dawei: Excuse me, where is the anatomy building?
  Student 2: The anatomy building is to the east of the library.
Ma Dawei: Where is the library?
  Student 2: It's behind the teaching building.
Ma Dawei: Thank you.
  Student 2: You are welcome.

生词 New words

1.	解剖楼	jiěpōulóu	n.	anatomy building
	解剖	jiěpōu	v.	to dissect
	楼	lóu	n.	building
2.	不好意思	bù hǎoyìsi		sorry
	意思	yìsi	n.	meaning
3.	知道	zhīdào	v.	to know, to be aware of
4.	别人	biérén	pron.	someone else
5.	地方	dìfang	n.	place
6.	图书馆	túshūguǎn	n.	library
7.	东边	dōngbian	n.	east
	东	dōng	n.	east
8.	教学楼	jiàoxuélóu	n.	teaching building
	教学	jiàoxué	v.	to teach
9.	后面	hòumiàn	n.	behind
	后	hòu	n.	behind, back

语言点 Language Points

动词重叠 "AA" 式　Verb-reduplication "AA" type

汉语中部分单音节动词可以重叠使用，重叠以后具有动作时间短或尝试的意义，重叠部分往往读轻声。例如：

Some monosyllabic verbs in Chinese can be reduplicated, which indicates that it lasts for a short time or it is for attempt. The reduplicated part is pronounced as the neutral tone. For example:

1. 你去问问（wènwen）别人吧。
2. 你看看（kànkan）这本书吧。
3. 星期天我想在家写写（xiěxie）作业，看看书。

第十一课　解剖楼在图书馆的东边
Lesson 11　The anatomy building is to the east of the library

※ 练习：请用所给动词的重叠形式完成对话　Please complete the dialogues with the reduplicative form of the given verbs

1. A：这本（běn，measure word for books）书怎么样？
   B：_____。（看）

2. A：请问，幸福小区在哪儿？
   B：_____。（问）

3. A：这个电影好吗？
   B：_____。（看）

4. A：星期六你做什么？
   B：_____。（写、玩儿）

综合练习 Comprehensive Exercises

一、根据汉字写拼音　Write Pinyin according to Chinese characters

1. 意思_____　　3. 解剖楼_____　　5. 知道_____
2. 别人_____　　4. 地方_____　　　6. 图书馆_____

二、朗读语句　Read aloud

1. 不好意思
2. 谢谢你
3. 不客气

4. 请问，图书馆在哪儿？
5. 图书馆在教学楼的后面。
6. 我明天想去图书馆。

三、替换练习 Substitution drills

1. 解剖楼 在什么地方？

> 医学院
> 图书馆
> 留学生宿舍

2. 请问 解剖楼 在哪儿？

> 教学楼
> 幸福小区
> 图书馆

3. 图书馆在 教学楼 的后面。

> 解剖楼
> 宿舍楼
> 医学院

四、选词填空 Use the following words to fill in the blanks

> 地方　知道　后面　别人　不好意思

1. 李真的家在什么_____？

2. 图书馆在教学楼的_____。

3. 我也不_____，你去问问老师吧。

4. _____，我不知道教学楼在哪儿。

5. 这些书都是_____的，不是我的。

五、根据课文内容回答问题 Answer the following questions according to the text

1. 马大为想去哪儿？
2. 解剖楼在什么地方？
3. 图书馆在哪儿？
4. 教学楼在哪儿？

六、根据课文内容填空 Fill in the blanks according to the text

马大为想去_____，他不知道_____。有个同学说_____在_____的东边，马大为_____不知道图书馆_____，别人说图书馆在教学楼的_____。

七、汉字书写 Write Chinese characters

楼	木 + 娄	一	十	十	木	术	术	栏	栏	样	样	楼	楼
意	音 + 心	丶	亠	立	立	产	音	音	音	音	意	意	
思	田 + 心	丨	冂	曰	田	田	思	思	思				
地	土 + 也	一	十	土	圵	地	地						
图	囗 + 冬	丨	冂	门	闪	冈	图	图					
东		一	七	车	东	东							

课文（二）
Text (Ⅱ)

(Class is begining, but Ma Dawei hasn't come to the classroom yet.)

Wáng lǎoshī: Mǎ Dàwéi zài nǎr?
王老师：马大为在哪儿？

Jīn Lóng: Lǎoshī, wǒ yě bù zhīdào, wǒ gěi tā dǎ diànhuà.
金龙：老师，我也不知道，我给他打电话。

(Jin Long is calling Ma Dawei.)

Jīn Lóng: Wèi, Dàwéi, wǒmen zài jiěpōulóu shàngkè. Nǐ zài nǎr ne?
金龙：喂，大为，我们在解剖楼上课。你在哪儿呢？

Mǎ Dàwéi: Wǒ yě bù zhīdào wǒ zài nǎr.
马大为：我也不知道我在哪儿。

Jīn Lóng: Nǐ zài xuéxiào lǐmiàn háishi wàimiàn?
金龙：你在学校里面还是外面？

Mǎ Dàwéi: Lǐmiàn.
马大为：里面。

Jīn Lóng: Nǐ de qiánmiàn shì shénme lóu?
金龙：你的前面是什么楼？

Mǎ Dàwéi: Wǒ kànkan. Qiánmiàn shì túshūguǎn, zuǒbian shì shíyànlóu, yòubian shì huāyuán.
马大为：我看看。前面是图书馆，左边是实验楼，右边是花园。

Jīn Lóng: Jiěpōulóu jiù zài túshūguǎn de dōngbian.
金龙：解剖楼就在图书馆的东边。

Mǎ Dàwéi: Kěshì, nǎbiān shì dōngbian ne?
马大为：可是，哪边是东边呢？

Teacher Wang: Where is Ma Dawei?
    Jin Long: I don't know, either. I'll call him.

Jin Long: Dawei, we are having class at the anatomy building. Where are you?
Ma Dawei: I don't know where I am.
    Jin Long: Are you inside or outside the school?
Ma Dawei: Inside.

Jin Long: What building is in front of you?

Ma Dawei: Let me see. The library is in front of me, the laboratory building is on the left and the garden on the right.

Jin Long: The anatomy building is just to the east of the library.

Ma Dawei: But, which side is the east?

生词 New words

1. 给	gěi	*prep.*	to, for
2. 打电话	dǎ diànhuà	*VO*	to make a call
打	dǎ	*v.*	to dial
3. 里面	lǐmiàn	*n.*	inside
4. 还是	háishi	*conj.*	or
5. 外面	wàimiàn	*n.*	outside
外	wài	*n.*	out
6. 前面	qiánmiàn	*n.*	ahead
7. 左边	zuǒbian	*n.*	leftside
左	zuǒ	*n.*	left
8. 实验楼	shíyànlóu	*n.*	the laboratory building
实验	shíyàn	*n./v.*	experiment; to test
9. 右边	yòubian	*n.*	rightside
右	yòu	*n.*	right
10. 花园	huāyuán	*n.*	garden
11. 就	jiù	*adv.*	exactly, precisely
12. 可是	kěshì	*conj.*	but, however

语言点 Language Points

一、方位名词 Locative noun

汉语中常用的方位名词有单纯方位词和合成方位词两种。单纯方位词包括"东、南、西（xī, west）、北（běi, north）、前、后、左、右、上（shàng, up）、下（xià, down）、里、外"等，多附着在名词后，很少单用。例如：

The commonly used locative nouns in Chinese include simple locative nouns and compound locative nouns. Simple locative nouns include "东、南、西（xī, west）、北（běi, north）、前、后、左、右、上（shàng, up）、下（xià, down）、里、外" and so on, which are mostly attached to nouns and rarely used alone. For example:

教室前　　解剖楼后　　桌子上

学校里　　教室外　　椅子下

合成方位词指在"东、南、西、北、前、后、左、右、上、下、里、外"等后加上词尾"边"或"面"构成的方位词，具体如下：

Compound locative nouns are formed by adding the suffix "边" or "面" after "东、南、西、北、前、后、左、右、上、下、里、外", as follows:

~边：东边　南边　西边　北边　前边　后边　左边　右边　上边　下边　里边　外边

~面：东面　南面　西面　北面　前面　后面　左面　右面　上面　下面　里面　外面

合成方位词一般用在"A＋在＋B（＋的）＋方位名词"结构中，其中"的"可以省略。例如：

Compound locative nouns are generally used in the structure of "A＋在＋B（＋的）＋locative noun", where "的" can be omitted. For example:

1. 解剖楼在图书馆的东边。

2. 宿舍在教室的北边。

3. 手机在桌子上面。

合成方位词还可用在"方位名词＋是＋地方名词"结构中。例如：

Compound locative nouns can also be used in the structure of "locative noun ＋ 是 ＋ place noun". For example:

4. 前面是图书馆，后面是花园。

5. 左边是解剖楼，右边是实验楼。

※ 练习：请用方位名词回答问题 Please answer the questions with locative nouns

1. 我们的教室在哪儿？
   _____。

2. 你的手机在哪儿？
   _____。

3. 谁在你的前边？
   _____。

4. 你后面的同学是谁？
   _____。

二、介词"给"　　Preposition "给"

介词"给"常与代词或名词组成介宾结构做状语，这里的代词或名词通常是指动作涉及的对象。例如：

The preposition "给" is often used with a pronoun or a noun to form a prepositional structure to act as an adverbial modifier. The pronoun or noun here usually refers to the object of the action. For example:

1. 我给他打电话。
2. 我给美丽买苹果。
3. 李老师给我们上课。

※ 练习：请用介词"给"回答问题 Please answer the questions with preposition "给"

1. 今天谁给你们上课？
   _____。

2. 今年谁给你过生日？
   _____。

3. 你今天给谁打电话？
   _____。

三、选择问句　Alternative question

汉语中的选择问句常用连词"还是"连接两种或两种以上的选项，要求对方从中选择一项。例如：

In the alternative question in Chinese, the conjunction "还是" is often used to connect two or more selections for the other one to choose from. For example:

1. 你在学校里面还是外面？
2. 你是老师还是学生？
3. 你哥哥在医院工作还是在学校工作？

※ 练习：请用连词"还是"完成对话　Please complete the dialogues with conjunction "还是"

1. A：_____？
   B：我住在宿舍里。
2. A：_____？
   B：我在家吃早饭。
3. A：_____？
   B：我学习医学（medical science）。
4. A：_____？
   B：我买苹果。

四、副词"就"（2）　Adverb "就" (2)

副词"就"在陈述句中可以强调肯定的语气，多用于口语，这时"就"往往重读。例如：

The adverb "就" can be used in declarative sentences to emphasize a positive tone, and it is mostly used in spoken language. In this case, "就" is often stressed. For example:

1. 解剖楼就在图书馆的东边。
2. 他就是马大为。
3. 哥哥就在这个医院工作。

※ 练习：请用副词"就"回答问题 Please answer the questions with adverb "就"

1. 你知道谁住在留学生宿舍吗？
   _____。

2. 谁是你们的老师？
   _____。

3. 你们的教室在哪儿？
   _____。

4. 医学院在哪儿？
   _____。

综合练习 Comprehensive Exercises

一、根据汉字写拼音 Write Pinyin according to Chinese characters

1. 还是_____   3. 前面_____   5. 左边_____

2. 可是_____   4. 外面_____   6. 右边_____

二、朗读语句 Read aloud

1. 超市（chāoshì, supermarket）
2. 银行（yínháng, bank）
3. 教室

4. 请问，超市在哪儿？
5. 超市在银行的前面。
6. 教室在图书馆后面。

三、替换练习 Substitution drills

1. 我给 <u>他</u> 打电话。

> 老师
> 金龙
> 妈妈

2. 你在 <u>学校</u> 里面还是外面？

> 实验楼
> 教学楼
> 图书馆

3. 你的 <u>前面</u> 是什么楼？

> 后面
> 左边
> 右边

四、选词填空 Use the following words to fill in the blanks

> 给　可是　还是　左边　就

1. 图书馆在教学楼的_____。

2. 你看，解剖楼_____在那儿！

3. 今天是星期六_____星期天？

4. 明天是妈妈的生日，你要_____她打电话吗？

5. 我很想去看电影，_____今天没有时间。

五、根据课文内容回答问题 Answer the following questions according to the text

1. 金龙知道马大为在哪儿吗？
2. 他们在哪儿上课？
3. 马大为在学校里面还是外面？
4. 马大为的前面是什么地方？

六、根据课文内容填空 Fill in the blanks according to the text

今天，金龙和马大为在_____上课，马大为不_____解剖楼在哪儿。他现在在学校里面，他的_____是图书馆，_____是实验楼，_____是花园。解剖楼_____在图书馆的东边。_____，马大为不知道哪边是东边。

七、汉字书写 Write Chinese characters

给	纟+合													
	乚	乡	纟	纠	纩	细	给	给						
打	扌+丁													
	一	十	扌	打	打									
左	ナ+工													
	一	ナ	左	左	左									
右	ナ+口													
	一	ナ	右	右	右									
花	艹+化													
	一	十	艹	艹	芒	芢	花	花						
园	囗+元													
	丨	冂	冂	厈	厈	园	园							

语言任务 Language Tasks

一、阅读理解 Reading comprehension

今天马大为在解剖楼有课，可是他不知道解剖楼在哪儿。现在，马大为的前面是图书馆，左边是实验楼，右边是花园。金龙说，解剖楼就在图书馆的东边。

读后判断 True or false

1. 马大为在图书馆的后面。　　　　　　　　　　　　　　（　　）
2. 图书馆在解剖楼的东边。　　　　　　　　　　　　　　（　　）
3. 马大为和金龙都不知道解剖楼在哪儿。　　　　　　　　（　　）

二、口头表达 Oral expression

任务名称：图书馆在哪儿？

Task: Where is the library?

任务要求：三名学生一组，互相询问学校图书馆的位置。

Requirements: Work in the group of three and ask about the location of the school library.

Reference words：里面　外面　左边　右边　前面　后面　还是　就　教学楼　解剖楼

第十一课　解剖楼在图书馆的东边

Lesson 11　The anatomy building is to the east of the library

第十二课 Lesson 12

Cài zuò de tài hǎochī le!
菜 做得 太好吃了！
The food is so delicious!

学习目标 Learning Objectives

1. Language Function: Order food.
2. Language Points: Imperative sentence (1); Modal verb "会" (1); Structural particle "得"; Adverb "有点儿"; Aspectual particle "了".

热身活动 Warming-up

1. 你知道这是什么菜吗？
Do you know what this dish is?

2. 你最喜欢吃的中国菜是什么？
What's your favorite Chinese food?

课文（一）
Text (1)

(Wang Dong, Wang Chen and Ma Dawei are in a restaurant.)

fúwùyuán: Xiānsheng, nín jǐ wèi?
服务员：先生，您几位？

Wáng Dōng: Sān wèi.
王东：三位。

fúwùyuán: Qǐng zuò.
服务员：请坐。

Wáng Dōng: Jīntiān wǒ qǐngkè.
王东：今天我请客。

Wáng Chén: Tài hǎo le! Wǒ diǎn Běijīng kǎoyā hé gōngbǎo jīdīng.
王晨：太好了！我点北京烤鸭和宫保鸡丁。

Mǎ Dàwéi: Wǒ zuì xǐhuan chī gōngbǎo jīdīng, měi gè xīngqī dōu chī.
马大为：我最喜欢吃宫保鸡丁，每个星期都吃。

Wáng Dōng: Nǐ huì zuò ma?
王东：你会做吗？

Mǎ Dàwéi: Wǒ bú huì zuò, kěshì wǒ huì dìng wàimài!
马大为：我不会做，可是我会订外卖！

Wáng Dōng: Wǒ yě cháng dìng wàimài.
王东：我也常订外卖。

Mǎ Dàwéi: Nín yě bú huì zuòfàn ma?
马大为：您也不会做饭吗？

Wáng Chén: Gēge huì zuòfàn, zuò de hěn hǎochī.
王晨：哥哥会做饭，做得很好吃。

Wáng Dōng: Wǒ xǐhuan zuòfàn, kěshì gōngzuò tài máng le, méi shíjiān zuò. Dàwéi, nǐ hē shénme?
王东：我喜欢做饭，可是工作太忙了，没时间做。大为，你喝什么？

Mǎ Dàwéi: Wǒ hē chá.
马大为：我喝茶。

Waiter: How many are you, Sir?
Wang Dong: Three.

第十二课 菜做得太好吃了！
Lesson 12 The food is so delicious!

Waiter: Please have a seat.
Wang Dong: It's my treat today.
Wang Chen: Great! I'll have Beijing roast duck and kung pao chicken.
Ma Dawei: My favorite dish is kung pao chicken! I eat it every week!
Wang Dong: Can you cook that?
Ma Dawei: No, I can't, but I can order a take-out!
Wang Dong: I often order take-outs!
Ma Dawei: You can't cook, either?
Wang Chen: My elder brother can cook and he cooks very well!
Wang Dong: I like cooking very much, but I am too busy to cook. What would you like to drink, Dawei?
Ma Dawei: I'd like tea.

生词 New words

1. 服务员	fúwùyuán	n.	waiter, waitress
2. 先生	xiānsheng	n.	Mr, sir
3. 位	wèi	m.	a measure word for people with respect
4. 请客	qǐngkè	v.	to treat, to invite sb. to dinner
5. 点	diǎn	v.	to order dishes
6. 北京烤鸭	Běijīng kǎoyā		Beijing Roast Duck
7. 宫保鸡丁	gōngbǎo jīdīng		spicy diced chicken, Kung Pao chicken
8. 会	huì	mod.v.	can, to be able to
9. 做	zuò	v.	to cook
10. 订外卖	dìng wàimài	VO	to order a takeaway
订	dìng	v.	to order
外卖	wàimài	n.	take-out, takeaway
11. 常	cháng	adv.	often, usually
12. 做饭	zuòfàn	v.	to cook, to prepare a meal
13. 得	de	part.	a structural particle, used after verbs or adjectives to connect complements of degree and result
14. 好吃	hǎochī	adj.	delicious
15. 喝	hē	v.	to drink
16. 茶	chá	n.	tea

专名 Proper nouns

1. 王东　　Wáng Dōng　　name of a Chinese doctor, Wang Chen's elder brother
2. 北京　　Běijīng　　　Beijing

语言点 Language Points

一、祈使句（1）　Imperative sentence (1)

"请"是汉语里常用的敬辞。让别人做某事时，动词前面加上"请"会让语气更礼貌。例如：

"请" is a commonly used polite expression in Chinese. When asking someone to do something, the speaker add "请" before the verb to make the tone sound more polite. For example:

1. 请坐。
2. 请喝茶。
3. 请喝水。

※ 练习：回答问题　Answer the question

当朋友到你家做客（to be a guest）时，你会对朋友说什么？

_____。

二、能愿动词"会"（1）　Modal verb "会" (1)

能愿动词"会"，可以表示通过学习掌握了某种技能。例如：

The modal verb "会" can indicate that a certain skill has been mastered through learning. For example:

1. 我会做饭。
2. 金龙会订外卖。
3. 马大为会手机支付。

第十二课　菜做得太好吃了！
Lesson 12　The food is so delicious!

其否定形式是在"会"前加"不"。例如：

Its negative form is to add "不" before "会". For example:

4. 我不会做饭。

5. 我不会写汉字（Hànzì, character）。

6. 我不会打电话。

※ 练习：请用能愿动词"会"回答问题 Please answer the questions with modal verb "会"

1. 你会做饭吗？
   _____。

2. 在你们家，谁最会做饭？
   _____。

3. 你会订外卖吗？
   _____。

4. 你会玩儿电脑游戏吗？
   _____。

三、结构助词"得"　Structural particle "得"

结构助词"得"用在动词和情态补语之间，其后的情态补语说明动作行为或事物性质所达到的状态。例如：

The structural particle "得" is used between verbs and modal complements. The following modal complements are used to describe the state of the action or the nature of things. For example:

1. 哥哥会做饭，做得很好吃。

2. 我会玩儿电脑游戏，玩儿得很好。

3. 这个宫保鸡丁做得不好吃。

※ 练习：回答问题　Answer the questions

1. 王老师的课上得怎么样？

   _____。

2. 你做饭做得怎么样？

   _____。

3. 你昨天睡得早吗？

   _____。

4. 你今天早饭吃得好吗？

   _____。

综合练习 Comprehensive Exercises

一、根据汉字写拼音 Write Pinyin according to Chinese characters

1. 请客_____　　3. 外卖_____　　5. 好吃_____

2. 先生_____　　4. 做饭_____　　6. 喝茶_____

二、朗读语句 Read aloud

1. 请坐
2. 订外卖
3. 做饭

4. 你会做饭吗？
5. 你汉语说得很好。
6. 你常去图书馆吗？

第十二课　菜做得太好吃了！
Lesson 12　The food is so delicious!

三、替换练习 Substitution drills

1. 我也常 <u>订外卖</u>。

> 去图书馆
> 看电影
> 坐公共汽车

2. 你会 <u>做饭</u> 吗?

> 说汉语
> 写汉字（Hànzì，Chinese character）
> 做宫保鸡丁

3. <u>饭</u> <u>做</u> 得 <u>很好吃</u>。

> 汉语
> 汉字
> 作业

> 说
> 写
> 做

> 非常好
> 很好看（hǎokàn，good-looking）
> 很对

四、选词填空 Use the following words to fill in the blanks

> 点　会　请　常　位

1. 老师，您_____坐!

2. 我想_____宫保鸡丁。

3. 你_____做北京烤鸭吗?

4. 我_____去朋友的学校玩儿。

5. 这_____是我的汉语老师，王老师。

五、根据课文内容回答问题 Answer the following questions according to the text

1. 今天谁请客？
2. 王晨点了什么？
3. 马大为最喜欢吃什么？
4. 王东会做饭吗？
5. 马大为想喝什么？

六、根据课文内容填空 Fill in the blanks according to the text

今天王东_____，王晨想_____北京烤鸭和宫保鸡丁。马大为_____喜欢吃宫保鸡丁，_____个星期都吃。马大为不会做，_____他会订外卖。王东也_____订外卖。王东很喜欢做饭，做_____很好吃，可是工作太_____了，没有_____做。

七、汉字书写 Write Chinese characters

先	生 + 儿
	ノ 一 十 生 先 先
位	亻 + 立
	ノ 亻 亻 亻 伫 位 位
会	人 + 云
	ノ 人 人 合 会 会
订	讠 + 丁
	丶 讠 讠 订 订
得	彳 + 䙷
	ノ 彳 彳 彳 彳 彳 得 得 得 得
喝	口 + 曷
	丨 口 口 叩 叩 叩 吗 吗 喝 喝 喝

课文（二）
Text (Ⅱ)

(Jin Long and Ma Dawei are chatting in the dorm.)

Jīn Lóng: Wǒmen qù tī zúqiú ba.
金龙：我们去踢足球吧。

Mǎ Dàwéi: Wǒ bú qù.
马大为：我不去。

Jīn Lóng: Wèi shénme?
金龙：为什么？

Mǎ Dàwéi: Wǒ dùzi yǒu diǎnr téng, zhōngwǔ chī de tài duō le.
马大为：我肚子有点儿疼，中午吃得太多了。

Jīn Lóng: Nǐmen chīle shénme?
金龙：你们吃了什么？

Mǎ Dàwéi: Wǒmen sān gè rén chīle liù gè cài, sān wǎn mǐfàn.
马大为：我们三个人吃了六个菜、三碗米饭。

Jīn Lóng: Nǐmen chī de tài duō le!
金龙：你们吃得太多了！

Mǎ Dàwéi: Fàndiàn de cài zuò de tài hǎochī le!
马大为：饭店的菜做得太好吃了！

Jīn Lóng: Nǎ gè fàndiàn?
金龙：哪个饭店？

Mǎ Dàwéi: Xuéxiào pángbiān de fàndiàn.
马大为：学校旁边的饭店。

Jin Long: Let's play soccer.

Ma Dawei: I don't want to go.

Jin Long: Why?

Ma Dawei: I have a stomachache. I ate too much this evening.

Jin Long: What did you eat?

Ma Dawei: The three of us eat six dishes and three bowls of rice.

Jin Long: You ate too much!

Ma Dawei: The food in that restaurant is so delicious!

Jin Long: Which restaurant?

Ma Dawei: The one near our school.

生词 New words

1. 踢足球　　　tī zúqiú　　　VO　　　to play football
   踢　　　　　tī　　　　　　v.　　　to kick
   足球　　　　zúqiú　　　　n.　　　football
2. 肚子　　　　dùzi　　　　　n.　　　abdomen
3. 有点儿　　　yǒudiǎnr　　　adv.　　a little bit
4. 了　　　　　le　　　　　　part.　　an aspectual particle to indicate the completion of an action
5. 菜　　　　　cài　　　　　　n.　　　dish
6. 碗　　　　　wǎn　　　　　n.　　　bowl
7. 米饭　　　　mǐfàn　　　　n.　　　cooked rice
8. 饭店　　　　fàndiàn　　　n.　　　restaurant
9. 旁边　　　　pángbiān　　　n.　　　beside

语言点 Language Points

一、副词"有点儿"　Adverb "有点儿"

副词"有点儿"常用在形容词前，表示程度不高，常用于不满意的事情。例如：

The adverb "有点儿" is often used in front of adjectives, indicating a low degree, and is often used for unsatisfactory things. For example:

1. 我肚子有点儿疼。
2. 他晚上吃得有点儿多。
3. 学校离我家有点儿远。
4. 住在学校宿舍有点儿不方便。

第十二课　菜做得太好吃了！
Lesson 12　The food is so delicious!

※ 练习：请用副词"有点儿"回答问题　Please answer the questions with adverb "有点儿"

1. 金龙今天高兴吗？
　　_____。

2. 你起床起得早吗？
　　_____。

3. 你一直在玩儿游戏，眼睛疼吗？
　　_____。

4. 你为什么不吃饭？
　　_____。

二、动态助词"了"　　Aspectual particle "了"

　　动态助词"了"用在动词之后，表示动作完成。"了"后面的宾语常常有数量短语修饰。例如：

The aspectual particle "了" is used after verbs to indicate the completion of the action. The object after "了" is often put after quantitative phrases. For example:

1. 我们吃了六个菜。

2. 我喝了两瓶水。

3. 我中午吃了两碗米饭。

※ 练习：请用动态助词"了"回答问题　Please answer the questions with aspectual particle "了"

1. 今天早上你吃了什么？
　　_____。

2. 昨天你买了什么？
　　_____。

3. 今天你喝了什么？
　　_____。

4. 过生日的时候，你做了什么？

_____。

综合练习 Comprehensive Exercises

一、根据汉字写拼音 Write Pinyin according to Chinese characters

1. 足球_____   3. 碗_____   5. 米饭_____

2. 饭店_____   4. 旁边_____   6. 菜_____

二、朗读语句 Read aloud

1. 三碗米饭
2. 四个菜
3. 肚子疼

4. 今天我肚子有点儿疼。
5. 我们三个人点了四个菜、三碗米饭。
6. 饭店的菜做得太好吃了！

三、替换练习 Substitution drills

1. 我们去 <u>踢足球</u> 吧。

上课
买水果
看电影

2. <u>我肚子</u> 有点儿 <u>疼</u>。

我　　　　　忙
这个苹果　　大
教室里的学生　多

第十二课　菜做得太好吃了！
Lesson 12　The food is so delicious!

3. 你们 吃 了什么?

> 买
> 做
> 喝

四、选词填空 Use the following words to fill in the blanks

> 踢 了 碗 旁边 有点儿

1. 我想要一_____米饭。

2. 你喜欢_____足球吗?

3. 中午你们吃_____什么?

4. 教室就在图书馆的_____。

5. 我今天_____累,想休息休息。

五、根据课文内容回答问题 Answer the following questions according to the text

1. 马大为为什么不去踢足球?

2. 马大为和朋友们吃了什么?

3. 他们中午在哪个饭店吃饭?

4. 饭店的菜做得怎么样?

六、根据课文内容填空 Fill in the blanks according to the text

金龙想和马大为去_____足球,可是马大为肚子_____疼。马大为、王晨和王东三个人中午吃_____六个_____、三_____米饭。马大为他们在学校_____的饭店吃的,那儿的菜做得太_____了。

七、汉字书写 Write Chinese characters

足	丶	口	口	甲	甲	足	足				
球	王+求										
	一	二	干	王	玗	坊	坊	玞	玞	球	球
菜	艹+采										
	一	十	艹	艹	苎	䒑	芇	苹	苹	茅	菜
碗	石+宛										
	一	丆	厂	石	石	石`	矿	矿	砚	砚	碗	碗
米	丶	丷	丷	半	米	米					
旁	产+方										
	丶	二	亠	亣	产	产	产	旁	旁		

语言任务 Language Tasks

一、阅读理解 Reading comprehension

今天王东在学校旁边的饭店请客，他请马大为、王晨和金龙一起吃饭。马大为非常喜欢吃宫保鸡丁，每个星期他都吃这个菜。王晨也喜欢吃宫保鸡丁，还很喜欢吃北京烤鸭。金龙也喜欢吃这两个菜。他们四个人吃了六个菜、四碗米饭。王东做饭很好吃，可是工作太忙了，没有时间做。

读后判断 True or false

1. 今天王晨请客。　　　　　　　　　　　　　　　　　　　（　）
2. 王东不会做饭。　　　　　　　　　　　　　　　　　　　（　）
3. 马大为、金龙和王晨都喜欢吃宫保鸡丁。　　　　　　　　（　）

二、口头表达 Oral expression

任务名称：今天我请客。

Task: It's my treat today.

任务要求：1. 三名学生一组，一起去饭店吃饭。

2. 点一些菜和饭，再点一些喝的，并说一说自己喜欢吃哪些菜。

Requirements: 1. Work in the group of three and go to a restaurant for dinner.

2. Order some dishes and drinks, and talk about which dishes you like.

Reference words: 点　菜　碗　米饭　宫保鸡丁　北京烤鸭　喝　茶　有点儿　得

第十三课 Lesson 13

Zhèr bù néng chōuyān
这儿不能抽烟
No smoking here

学习目标 Learning Objectives

1. Language Function: Express permission.
2. Language Points: Numeral measure word "一下"; Adverb "马上"; Modal verb "能" (1); Modal verb "要" (1); Locative noun "以后".

热身活动 Warming-up

1. 我们经常在哪儿看到这个标志?
   Where do we usually see this sign?

2. 你知道抽烟有哪些坏处吗?
   What disadvantages do you know about smoking?

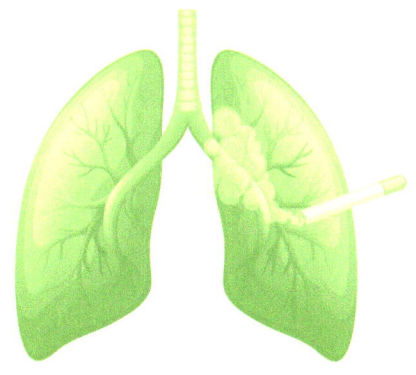

课文（一）
Text（Ⅰ）

(The patient's family member is smoking in the ward.)

hùshi: Sān chuáng bìngrén de jiāshǔ zài ma? Qǐng qù yíxià yīshēng bàngōngshì.
护士：三　床　病人的家属在吗？请去一下医生　办公室。

bìngrén jiāshǔ: Wǒ jiù shì, mǎshàng qù.
病人家属：我　就是，马上　去。

hùshi: Xiānsheng, zhèr bù néng chōuyān.
护士：先生，　这儿不能　抽烟。

bìngrén jiāshǔ: Bù hǎoyìsi, wǒ qù wàibian chōu.
病人家属：不好意思，我去外边　抽。

hùshi: Wàibian yě bùxíng.
护士：外边　也不行。

bìngrén jiāshǔ: Wèishēngjiān li xíng ma?
病人家属：卫生间　里行吗？

hùshi: Bùxíng. Zhèr shì yīyuàn, bù néng chōuyān.
护士：不行。这儿是医院，不能　抽烟。

bìngrén jiāshǔ: Duìbuqǐ.
病人家属：对不起。

Nurse: Is the family member of Bed 3 here? Please go to the doctor's office.
Patient's family: I am. I will go immediately.
Nurse: Sir, no smoking here!
Patient's family: Sorry, I will go out.
Nurse: No smoking outside, either.
Patient's family: Can I smoke in the bathroom?
Nurse: No. It is the hospital here. No smoking!
Patient's family: Sorry.

生词 New words

1. 病人	bìngrén	n.	patient
2. 家属	jiāshǔ	n.	family member

3. 一下	yíxià	num.-m.	once
4. 办公室	bàngōngshì	n.	office
5. 马上	mǎshàng	adv.	immediately
6. 这儿	zhèr	pron.	here
7. 能	néng	mod.v.	can
8. 抽烟	chōuyān	v.	to smoke (a cigarette or a pipe)
抽	chōu	v.	to smoke
烟	yān	n.	tobacco, cigarette
9. 不行	bùxíng	v.	to be not allowed
行	xíng	v.	to be all right
10. 卫生间	wèishēngjiān	n.	bathroom

语言点 Language Points

一、数量词"一下" Numeral measure word "一下"

数量词"一下"常放在动词后表示做一次或尝试着做某事。例如：

The numeral measure word "一下" is often placed after a verb, meaning to do once or try to do something. For example:

1. 病人家属，请去一下医生办公室。

2. 请问一下，解剖楼在哪儿？

3. 我想玩儿一下电脑，可以吗？

※ 练习：请用数量词"一下"完成句子 Please complete the sentences with numeral measure word "一下"

1. 马大为为什么没来上课？金龙你_____。

2. 这个汉字我不会写，你可以_____吗？

3. 现在几点了？你_____。

4. 这个电影非常有意思，你可以_____。

二、副词"马上"　　Adverb "马上"

副词"马上"表示动作行为或事情即将发生。例如：

The adverb "马上" indicates that an action or something is about to happen. For example:

1. 我马上去医生办公室。

2. 请你马上去一下老师的办公室。

3. 7：55，马上就上课了。

※ 练习：请用副词"马上"回答问题　Please answer the questions with adverb "马上"

1. A：你们什么时候到？
   B：_____。

2. A：现在9：50，你几点上课？
   B：_____。

3. A：你今天晚上几点睡觉？
   B：_____。

4. A：我的肚子很疼。
   B：_____。

三、能愿动词"能"（1）　　Modal verb "能" (1)

能愿动词"能"可以表示允许，常常用在疑问句和否定句中。例如：

The modal verb "能" expresses permission and is often used in interrogative sentences and negative sentences. For example:

1. 这儿能抽烟吗？

2. 这儿不能抽烟。

3. 在公共汽车上不能吃东西。

4. 上课不能睡觉。

※ 练习：请用能愿动词"能"完成对话 Please complete the dialogues with modal verb "能"

1. A：宿舍楼里能抽烟吗？
   B：_____。
2. A：_____？
   B：上课的时候不能玩儿手机。
3. A：上汉语课的时候能说英语（Yīngyǔ, English）吗？
   B：_____。

综合练习 Comprehensive Exercises

一、根据汉字写拼音 Write Pinyin according to Chinese characters

1. 病人_____   3. 办公室_____   5. 这儿_____
2. 马上_____   4. 抽烟_____   6. 卫生间_____

二、朗读语句 Read aloud

1. 看一下
2. 说一下
3. 写一下
4. 这儿不能抽烟。
5. 上课的时候不能睡觉。
6. 你能说一下你的名字吗？

三、替换练习 Substitution drills

1. 请去一下 <u>医生办公室</u>。

   教室
   图书馆
   608 房间

第十三课　这儿不能抽烟
Lesson 13　No smoking here

2. 这儿不能 抽烟。

> 睡觉
> 踢足球
> 打电话

3. 我去外边 抽。

> 看书
> 买水果
> 踢足球

四、选词填空 Use the following words to fill in the blanks

> 一下　能　行　马上　这儿

1. 请你来_____我的房间。

2. 我现在_____去你家。

3. 我_____去外边抽烟吗?

4. 去外边抽烟也不_____。

5. 你在_____做什么?

五、根据课文内容回答问题 Answer the following questions according to the text

1. 护士请三床病人的家属去哪儿?

2. 这儿能抽烟吗?

3. 外边能抽烟吗?

4. 卫生间里能抽烟吗?

5. 这儿为什么不能抽烟?

六、根据课文内容填空 Fill in the blanks according to the text

护士请三床病人的_____去一下_____，病人家属说_____。护士告诉（gàosu, tell）他这儿_____抽烟，他想去外边抽。护士说外边也_____，医院里都不能抽烟。

七、汉字书写 Write Chinese characters

病	疒+丙 丶 一 广 广 疒 疒 疒 病 病 病
办	丁 力 力 办
马	丁 马 马
能	肯+匕 ㄥ ㄙ ㄅ 台 台 育 肯 能 能 能
行	彳+丁 丿 彳 彳 彳 彳 行
卫	丁 卫 卫

课文（二）
Text（II）

(A doctor is talking with a patient's family member in the office.)

bìngrén jiāshǔ: Yīshēng nín hǎo, wǒ shì sān chuáng de jiāshǔ.
病人家属：医生 您好，我是三 床 的家属。

yīshēng: Míngtiān zǎoshang bā diǎn, sān chuáng zuò lánwěiyán shǒushù.
医生：明天 早上 八点，三 床 做 阑尾炎 手术。

bìngrén jiāshǔ: Wǒmen yào zhǔnbèi shénme?
病人家属：我们 要 准备 什么？

yīshēng: Jīntiān wǎnshang shídiǎn yǐhòu, bìngrén bù néng chī dōngxi, bù néng
医生：今天 晚上 十点以后，病人不能 吃 东西，不能
hē shuǐ. Míngtiān zǎoshang yě bù néng chī zǎofàn.
喝水。明天 早上 也不能 吃早饭。

bìngrén jiāshǔ: Hái yào zhǔnbèi shénme?
病人家属：还 要 准备 什么？

yīshēng: Búyòng zhǔnbèi biéde, zhè shì gè xiǎo shǒushù.
医生：不用 准备 别的，这是个小 手术。

bìngrén jiāshǔ: Xièxie nín.
病人家属：谢谢 您。

Patient's family: Doctor, I'm the family of the Bed 3.
    Doctor: The patient of Bed 3 will have an appendicitis operation at eight o'clock tomorrow morning.
Patient's family: What do we need to prepare?
    Doctor: The patient mustn't eat or drink after ten o'clock this evening and mustn't eat breakfast tomorrow morning.
Patient's family: What else?
    Doctor: You don't need to prepare anything else. This is a minor surgery.
Patient's family: Thank you.

生词 New words

1. 做手术	zuò shǒushù	*VO*	to have an operation
手术	shǒushù	*n.*	operation

2. 阑尾炎	lánwěiyán	n.	appendicitis
3. 要	yào	mod.v.	must, should
4. 准备	zhǔnbèi	v.	to prepare
5. 以后	yǐhòu	n.	after
6. 东西	dōngxi	n.	thing
7. 早饭	zǎofàn	n.	breakfast
8. 不用	búyòng	adv.	need not
用	yòng	v.	to need
9. 小	xiǎo	adj.	small

语言点 Language Points

一、能愿动词"要"（1） Modal verb "要" (1)

能愿动词"要"可以表示需要、应该做某事，其否定形式为"不用"。例如：

The modal verb "要" indicates that something needs to or should be done. The negative form is usually "不用". For example:

1. 我们要准备什么？

2. 上课的时候，我们要说汉语。

3. A：你去学校要坐公共汽车吗？

   B：我家离学校非常近，不用坐公共汽车。

4. A：她要每天工作吗？

   B：她有很多钱，不用工作。

5. A：明天你们要上课吗？

   B：明天星期六，我们不用去上课。

※ 练习：请用能愿动词"要"完成对话 Please complete the dialogues with modal verb "要"

1. A：_____？

   B：我们要准备面包和水。

2. A：_____？

   B：医生说不用做手术。

3. A：在中国学习医学，要学习汉语吗？

   B：_____。

二、方位名词"以后" Locative noun "以后"

方位名词"以后"表示现在或所说的某一个时间之后的时期。例如：

The locative noun "以后" means a certain time after now or some time mentioned. For example:

1. 今天晚上十点以后，病人不能吃东西，不能喝水。

2. 晚上十一点以后，我要休息。

3. 以后，我想学习做中国菜。

※ 练习：组词成句 Group words into sentences

1. 踢足球 去 以后 下课 我们

   _____。

2. 吃饭 不能 踢足球 以后 马上

   _____。

3. 手术 以后 休息 要 你

   _____。

4. 早睡觉 以后 我 想

   _____。

综合练习 Comprehensive Exercises

一、根据汉字写拼音 Write Pinyin according to Chinese characters

1. 早饭_____   3. 以后_____   5. 东西_____

2. 准备_____   4. 手术_____   6. 不用_____

二、朗读语句 Read aloud

1. 不能吃饭
2. 不能喝水
3. 不能抽烟
4. 明天早上不能吃早饭。
5. 明天早上你要做手术。
6. 晚上十点以后不能吃东西。

三、替换练习 Substitution drills

1. 晚上十点以后，病人不能 <u>吃东西</u>。

喝水
喝茶
吃水果

2. 还要 <u>准备</u> 什么？

3. 不用 <u>准备</u> 别的。

四、选词填空 Use the following words to fill in the blanks

东西　准备　以后　不用　马上

1. 你还想买_____吗？
2. 今天我订了外卖，你_____做饭。

3. 病人家属，现在_____去一下医生办公室。

4. 手术前我们要_____什么？

5. 明天有手术，你晚上十点_____不能吃东西，也不能喝水。

五、根据课文内容回答问题 Answer the following questions according to the text

1. 三床病人什么时候做手术？

2. 病人要做什么手术？

3. 手术前要准备什么？

4. 这是个大手术还是小手术？

六、根据课文内容填空 Fill in the blanks according to the text

医生告诉三床病人的_____，明天上午八点病人要_____手术。病人今天晚上十点_____不能吃_____，也不能_____。明天早上也不能吃_____。医生说这是个小手术，不用_____别的。

七、汉字书写 Write Chinese characters

手	一	二	三	手						
术	一	十	才	木	术					
准	冫+隹									
	、	冫	冫	冫	冫	泎	泎	浐	淮	准
备	夂+田									
	丿	夂	夂	冬	各	各	备	备		
用	丿	冂	月	月	用					
小	亅	小	小							

语言任务 Language Tasks

一、阅读理解 Reading comprehension

三床病人明天早上要做阑尾炎手术,医生说今天晚上十点以后,病人不能吃东西,不能喝水,明天早上也不能吃早饭。阑尾炎手术是个小手术。

读后判断 True or false

1. 三床病人明天做手术。 ( )
2. 病人明天可以吃早饭。 ( )
3. 今天晚上十点以后,病人不能吃东西,能喝水。 ( )

二、口头表达 Oral expression

任务名称:手术前的准备。

Task: Pre-surgery preparation.

任务要求:1. 两名学生一组,一名是病人家属,一名是医生。
　　　　　2. 病人家属向医生询问手术前的准备。

Requirements: 1. Work in a group of two. One acts as a family of the patient and the other acts as a doctor.
　　　　　　　2. The family asks about preparations before surgery.

Reference words: 做手术　以后　能　不用　别的　吃东西　喝水

第十三课　这儿不能抽烟
Lesson 13　No smoking here

第十四课 Lesson 14

Zhè jiàn báidàguà shì shéi de?
这 件 白大褂 是 谁 的?
Whose white coat is this?

学习目标 Learning Objectives

1. Language Function: Describe colors of items.
2. Language Points: Positive and negative question; "的" phrase; Existential sentence; Adverb "一定".

热身活动 Warming-up

1. 你喜欢什么颜色?
   What color do you like?

2. 你们国家的国旗上有什么颜色?
   What colors does your national flag have?

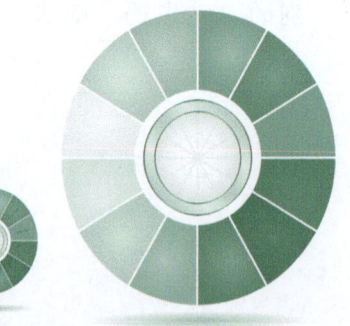

课文（一）
Text（I）

(Yueliang is shopping for clothes online.)

Yuèliang: Wǒ xiǎng mǎi qúnzi, zhè tiáo hǎokàn bu hǎokàn?
月亮：我想买裙子，这条好看不好看？

Měilì: Hěn hǎokàn, hái yǒu biéde yánsè ma?
美丽：很好看，还有别的颜色吗？

Yuèliang: Yǒu hěn duō yánsè, hēisè、lánsè、lǜsè, hái yǒu hóngsè hé huángsè, nǎ zhǒng yánsè hǎokàn?
月亮：有很多颜色，黑色、蓝色、绿色，还有红色和黄色，哪种颜色好看？

Měilì: Lán de hé hóng de dōu búcuò.
美丽：蓝的和红的都不错。

Yuèliang: Wǒ de hóng yīfu hěn shǎo, mǎi hóng de ba.
月亮：我的红衣服很少，买红的吧。

Měilì: Yǒu méiyǒu xiǎohào de?
美丽：有没有小号的？

Yuèliang: Yǒu.
月亮：有。

Yueliang: I want to buy a skirt. How about this one?
　Meili: Very beautiful! Any other colors?
Yueliang: There are many colors, black, blue, green, red and yellow. Which color looks better?
　Meili: I think both blue and red are good.
Yueliang: My red clothes are less. I'll buy a red one.
　Meili: Is there a small size?
Yueliang: Yes, there is.

生词 New words

1. 裙子　　qúnzi　　n.　　skirt
2. 条　　　tiáo　　　m.　　a measure word for slender things
3. 好看　　hǎokàn　 adj.　 beautiful, good-looking

4. 颜色	yánsè	n.	color
5. 黑色	hēisè	n.	black
黑	hēi	adj.	black
6. 蓝色	lánsè	n.	blue
蓝	lán	adj.	blue
7. 绿色	lǜsè	n.	green
绿	lǜ	adj.	green
8. 红色	hóngsè	n.	red
红	hóng	adj.	red
9. 黄色	huángsè	n.	yellow
黄	huáng	adj.	yellow
10. 种	zhǒng	m.	kind, sort
11. 不错	búcuò	adj.	good, not bad
12. 衣服	yīfu	n.	clothes
13. 少	shǎo	adj.	less, few
14. 小号	xiǎohào	adj.	small size

语言点 Language Points

一、正反疑问句 Positive and negative question

正反疑问句是由谓语的肯定形式和否定形式并列构成的疑问句。使用正反疑问句时，说话人一般急切地想知道答案，希望对方做出肯定或者否定的回答。例如：

Positive and negative questions are interrogative sentences formed by positive and negative forms of the predicate. When using positive and negative questions, the speaker is usually eager to know the answer and expects the other one to answer positively or negatively. For example:

1. 我想买裙子，这条好看不好看？
2. 你的手机贵不贵？

3. 这条裙子有没有小号的？

4. 星期六你休息不休息？

※ 练习：请用正反疑问句改写下列句子 Please rewrite the following sentences with positive and negative question

1. 这儿能抽烟吗？
   _____？

2. 你的红裙子多吗？
   _____？

3. 留学生宿舍楼远吗？
   _____？

4. 下课以后，你去图书馆吗？
   _____？

二、"的"字短语　"的" phrase

名词、代词、形容词和动词的后面加上"的"后可以组成"的"字短语。"的"字短语相当于一个名词性结构，被省略的中心语可以在上下文语境中明确。例如：

"的" can be added to nouns, pronouns, adjectives, and verbs to form the "的" phrase. "的" phrase is equivalent to a nominal structure. The omitted central word can be clarified in the context. For example:

1. 这本书不是月亮的，是老师的。

2. 这个手机不是我的。

3. A：你喜欢哪条裙子？
   B：蓝的和红的都不错。

4. 我想买条裙子，有没有小号的？

5. 你想买什么吃的？

※ 练习：请用"的"字短语改写下列句子 Please rewrite the following sentences with "的" phrase

1. 我喜欢红裙子，不喜欢黄裙子。
   _____。

2. 这是哥哥的手机，不是我的手机。
   _____。

3. 美丽的裙子是小号的裙子。
   _____。

4. 我想买黑色的手机，不想买红色的手机。
   _____。

综合练习 Comprehensive Exercises

一、根据汉字写拼音 Write Pinyin according to Chinese characters

1. 裙子_____   3. 颜色_____   5. 衣服_____

2. 好看_____   4. 不错_____   6. 小号_____

二、朗读语句 Read aloud

1. 买衣服
2. 一条裙子
3. 很多颜色

4. 你最喜欢什么颜色？
5. 我最喜欢蓝色。
6. 你想买什么颜色的衣服？

三、替换练习 Substitution drills

1. 这条裙子 好看不好看？

> 大不大
> 贵不贵
> 小不小

2. 蓝的 和 红的 都不错。

3. 有没有 小号的？

> 大号的
> 黑色的
> 蓝色的

四、选词填空 Use the following words to fill in the blanks

> 条　不　不错　少　种

1. 我想买一_____红色的裙子。

2. 这条裙子好看_____好看？

3. 你喜欢哪一_____颜色？

4. 你的汉语说得真_____。

5. 一个面包太_____了，我想吃两个。

五、根据课文内容回答问题 Answer the following questions according to the text

1. 月亮想买什么？

2. 裙子有哪些颜色？

3. 美丽说哪种颜色好看？

4. 红色的裙子有小号的吗？

六、根据课文内容填空 Fill in the blanks according to the text

月亮在网上（wǎngshàng，online）买衣服，她想买一_____裙子。裙子有很多_____，_____色、_____色、_____色、_____色、_____色都有。美丽觉得红_____和蓝_____都_____，红的有_____的。

七、汉字书写 Write Chinese characters

条	夂+朩	丿	夂	冬	冬	条	条						
颜	彦+页	丶	亠	六	产	立	产	产	彦	彦	彦	颜	颜
		颜											
色	夕+巴	丿	夕	夂	冬	争	色						
红	纟+工	乙	幺	纟	纟	红	红						
种	禾+中	一	二	千	禾	禾	禾	和	和	种			
衣		丶	亠	广	亣	衣	衣						

课文（二）
Text (Ⅱ)

(Jin Long saw two white coats in the laboratory.)

Jīn Lóng: Zhuōzi shàng yǒu liǎng jiàn báidàguà, zhè jiàn shì wǒ de, nà jiàn shì nǐ de ma?
金龙：桌子 上 有 两 件 白大褂，这件是我的，那件是你的吗？

Měilì: Bú shì wǒ de, wǒ de hěn xīn, zhè jiàn yǒudiǎnr jiù.
美丽：不是我的，我的很新，这件有点儿旧。

Jīn Lóng: Shì bu shì Yuèliang de?
金龙：是不是月亮的？

Měilì: Bú shì. Yuèliang chuān xiǎohào de, zhè jiàn shì dàhào de.
美丽：不是。月亮 穿 小号的，这件是大号的。

Jīn Lóng: Yídìng shì Mǎ Dàwéi de!
金龙：一定是马大为的！

Měilì: Zhuōzi shàng hái yǒu shūbāo, bǐjìběn, bēizi hé wǔ jiǎo qián, shì shéi de?
美丽：桌子 上 还有书包、笔记本、杯子和五角钱，是谁的？

Jīn Lóng: Wǒ kàn yíxià, shì Mǎ Dàwéi de zì, zhèxiē yě shì tā de.
金龙：我看一下，是马大为的字，这些也是他的。

Jin Long: There are two white coats on the desk. One is mine. Is the other one yours?
   Meili: It's not mine. Mine is new. This one is a bit old.
Jin Long: Is it Yueliang's?
   Meili: It's not hers. Yueliang's is a small one and this one is a large one.
Jin Long: It must belong to Ma Dawei.
   Meili: Whose bag, notebook, cup and five *mao* are on the desk?
Jin Long: Let me have a look. It is Ma Dawei's handwriting. All of these are his.

生词 New words

1.	上	shàng	n.	up, upward
2.	件	jiàn	m.	piece
3.	白大褂	báidàguà	n.	white coat
4.	新	xīn	adj.	new
5.	旧	jiù	adj.	old

6. 穿	chuān	v.	to wear
7. 大号	dàhào	adj.	large-size
8. 一定	yídìng	adv.	must
9. 书包	shūbāo	n.	bag
10. 笔记本	bǐjìběn	n.	notebook
11. 杯子	bēizi	n.	cup
12. 角	jiǎo	m.	*jiao*, a fractional unit of money in China, 1/10 of a *yuan*
13. 字	zì	n.	handwriting
14. 这些	zhèxiē	pron.	these

语言点 Language Points

一、存在句（1） Existential sentence (1)

汉语中表示某处存在某物的句子叫存在句，其常用结构是"处所名词＋有＋数量词＋事物名词"，即"N处所＋有＋Num-M＋N"。例如：

In Chinese, a sentence that expresses the existence of something in a certain place is called an existential sentence. Its common structure is "location noun + 有 + numeral measure word + thing noun", that is, "N处所 + 有 + Num-M + N". For example:

1. 桌子上有两件白大褂。
2. 床上有一条裙子。
3. 图书馆里有很多书。

※ 练习：组词成句 Group words into sentences

1. 三个　教室　里　留学生　有

_____。

2. 花园　小区　两个　里　有

_____。

3. 桌子　有　上　一个　杯子

   _____。

4. 椅子　一件　上　有　红裙子

   _____。

二、副词"一定"　Adverb "一定"

副词"一定"表示必定、确定，常用在动词、形容词的前边。例如：

The adverb "一定" means "certainly", "definitely", and is often used before verbs and adjectives. For example:

1. 这件白大褂一定是马大为的！
2. 他没来上课，一定是在宿舍睡觉。
3. 你哥哥是医生，他工作一定很忙。

"一定"也可以表示态度很坚决，此时常跟能愿动词"要"搭配使用。例如：

"一定" can also mean a firm attitude. At this time, it's often used with modal verb "要". For example:

4. 我一定要早睡早起。
5. 你一定不要抽烟。

※ 练习：请用副词"一定"改写下列句子 Please rewrite the following sentences with adverb "一定"

1. A：医生的工作很忙吧？
   B：_____。

2. A：这个菜是谁做的？很好吃！
   B：_____。

3. A：金龙为什么没来？
   B：_____。

4. A：明天下午你去踢足球吗？
   B：_____。

综合练习 Comprehensive Exercises

一、根据汉字写拼音 Write Pinyin according to Chinese characters

1. 穿_____ 3. 一定_____ 5. 旧_____

2. 新_____ 4. 件_____ 6. 杯子_____

二、朗读语句 Read aloud

1. 一件新衣服
2. 一件旧衣服
3. 一件白大褂

4. 桌子上有什么？
5. 桌子上有很多书。
6. 这件衣服有点儿旧。

三、替换练习 Substitution drills

1. 桌子上有 <u>两件白大褂</u>。

   一个书包
   一个杯子
   一个笔记本

2. 这些东西是不是 <u>月亮的</u>？

   马大为的
   王老师的
   你哥哥的

3. 月亮穿 <u>小号的</u>。

   大号的
   红色的
   蓝色的

四、选词填空 Use the following words to fill in the blanks

> 件　新　上　一定　穿

1. 桌子_____有什么东西？

2. 我今天_____要去看他。

3. 我的书包太旧了，我要买一个_____的。

4. 你知道妈妈_____什么号的衣服吗？

5. 每个学生都有一_____白大褂。

五、根据课文内容回答问题 Answer the following questions according to the text

1. 桌子上有什么？

2. 那件白大褂是谁的？

3. 桌子上还有什么？

4. 桌子上的这些东西都是谁的？

六、根据课文内容填空 Fill in the blanks according to the text

桌子上有_____白大褂，一件是金龙的，还有一件不知道是_____。美丽的白大褂很_____，那件有点儿_____。那件也不是_____的，月亮_____小号的，那件是_____的。金龙说_____是马大为的。桌子上的书包、_____、杯子和五_____钱也是马大为的。

七、汉字书写 Write Chinese characters

件	亻+牛										
	丿	亻	亻	仁	仁	件					
白	丿	亻	白	白	白						
新	亲+斤										
	丶	丄	亠	辛	立	立	辛	辛	亲	亲	新	新	新
旧	丨+日										
	丨	丨丨	丬丨	旧	旧						
穿	穴+牙										
	丶	丷	宀	宀	穴	空	穿	穿			
定	宀+疋										
	丶	丷	宀	宀	宇	宇	定	定			

语言任务 Language Tasks

一、阅读理解 Reading comprehension

这是美丽的房间：房间里的床上有两条裙子，一条是蓝色的，一条是黑色的；椅子上有一件白大褂，白大褂有点儿大，还有点儿旧；桌子上有一个杯子、一瓶水和一个笔记本。

读后判断 True or false

1. 美丽的裙子在椅子上。　　　　　　　　　　　　　　　　　（　　）

2. 那件白大褂是新的。　　　　　　　　　　　　　　　　　　（　　）

3. 美丽的桌子上有很多东西。　　　　　　　　　　　　　　　（　　）

二、口头表达 Oral expression

任务名称：你喜欢哪一件衣服？

Task: Which one do you like?

任务要求：1. 三名学生一组，两名是一起来买衣服的顾客，另外一名是售货员。

2. 互相询问颜色喜好、价格和尺码。

Requirements: 1. Work in a group of three. Two acts as customers who come together to buy clothes, and another acts as a shop assistant.

2. Ask each other about color preference, price and size.

Reference words: 颜色　红的　蓝的　黑的　绿的　种　裙子　衣服　件　条　穿　大号　小号

第十五课 Lesson 15

Tiān qíng le
天 晴 了
The sky clears up

学习目标 Learning Objectives

1. Language Function: Describe the weather and ask about preferences.
2. Language Points: Modal particle "了"; Interrogative pronoun "怎么"; Numeral measure word "一点儿"; Modal verb "会" (2).

热身活动 Warming-up

1. 你喜欢哪种天气?
   Which weather do you like?

2. 你喜欢什么运动?
   What sports do you like?

课文（一）
Text（I）

(Ma Dawei asked Wang Chen to go to climb the mountain.)

Mǎ Dàwéi: Tiān qíng le, wǒmen qù pá shān, zěnmeyàng?
马大为：天晴了，我们去爬山，怎么样？

Wáng Chén: Hǎo a.
王晨：好啊。

Mǎ Dàwéi: Nǐ gēge yě qù ma? Tā yǒu chē, kěyǐ kāichē qù.
马大为：你哥哥也去吗？他有车，可以开车去。

Wáng Chén: Tā bú qù, tā xiàwǔ yǒu shǒushù.
王晨：他不去，他下午有手术。

Mǎ Dàwéi: Wǒmen zuò chūzūchē qù ba.
马大为：我们坐出租车去吧。

Wáng Chén: Zuò chūzūchē yǒudiǎnr guì, qí zìxíngchē qù zěnmeyàng?
王晨：坐出租车有点儿贵，骑自行车去怎么样？

Mǎ Dàwéi: Kěshì wǒ méiyǒu zìxíngchē.
马大为：可是我没有自行车。

Wáng Chén: Méishìr, wǒmen kěyǐ qí gòngxiǎng dānchē.
王晨：没事儿，我们可以骑共享单车。

Mǎ Dàwéi: Gòngxiǎng dānchē zěnme yòng?
马大为：共享单车怎么用？

Wáng Chén: Fēicháng jiǎndān, wǒ jiāo nǐ.
王晨：非常简单，我教你。

Ma Dawei: It's sunny. Let's go climbing the mountain, shall we?
Wang Chen: OK.
Ma Dawei: Will your brother go with us? He can drive his car.
Wang Chen: He won't go. He has a surgery this afternoon.
Ma Dawei: Let's take a taxi.
Wang Chen: It's a bit expensive to take a taxi. How about riding a bike?
Ma Dawei: But I have no bike.
Wang Chen: It doesn't matter. We can ride shared bikes.
Ma Dawei: How to use shared bikes?
Wang Chen: It's very simple. I'll teach you.

第十五课　天晴了
Lesson 15　The sky clears up

生词 New words

1. 晴	qíng	*adj.*	sunny, clear	
2. 爬山	pá shān	*VO*	to climb mountains	
爬	pá	*v.*	to climb	
山	shān	*n.*	mountain	
3. 车	chē	*n.*	car	
4. 开车	kāichē	*v.*	to drive	
开	kāi	*v.*	to drive, to operate	
5. 出租车	chūzūchē	*n.*	taxi	
6. 骑	qí	*v.*	to ride	
7. 自行车	zìxíngchē	*n.*	bike	
8. 没事儿	méishìr	*v.*	it doesn't matter; that's all right	
9. 共享单车	gòngxiǎng dānchē		shared bike	
共享	gòngxiǎng	*v.*	to share	
单车	dānchē	*n.*	bike	
10. 怎么	zěnme	*pron.*	how	
11. 用	yòng	*v.*	to use	
12. 简单	jiǎndān	*adj.*	easy, simple	
13. 教	jiāo	*v.*	to teach	

语言点 Language Points

一、语气助词"了"（1） Modal particle "了" (1)

语气助词"了"一般用在句尾，表示情况出现了变化。例如：

The modal particle "了" is usually used at the end of a sentence to indicate that the situation has changed. For example:

1. 天晴了。

2. 上课了！

3. 他的肚子不疼了。

※ 练习：组词成句 Group words into sentences

1. 抽烟　不　他　了

   _____。

2. 我的　好　阑尾炎　了

   _____。

3. 马大为　了　不　今天　来

   _____。

4. 哥哥　了　工作　不忙　的

   _____。

二、疑问代词"怎么"（1）　Interrogative pronoun "怎么" (1)

疑问代词"怎么"常用来询问方式、原因等。例如：

The interrogative pronoun "怎么" is often used to ask how, why, etc. For example:

1. 共享单车怎么用？
2. 我们怎么去爬山？
3. 他怎么没来上课？

※ 练习：请用疑问代词"怎么"完成对话　Please complete the dialogues with interrogative pronoun "怎么"

1. A：_____？

   B：我骑自行车去学校。

2. A：_____？

   B：哥哥坐公共汽车去医院。

3. A：_____？

   B：我用手机订外卖。

4. A：_____？

   B：他一定在房间睡觉。

第十五课　天晴了

Lesson 15　The sky clears up

综合练习 Comprehensive Exercises

一、根据汉字写拼音 Write Pinyin according to Chinese characters

1. 晴_____   3. 没事儿_____   5. 爬山_____

2. 出租车_____   4. 怎么_____   6. 自行车_____

二、朗读语句 Read aloud

1. 开车
2. 坐出租车
3. 骑自行车

4. 坐出租车有点儿贵。
5. 骑自行车很方便。
6. 我们可以开车去学校。

三、替换练习 Substitution drills

1. 我们去 爬山，怎么样？

吃饭
看电影
踢足球

2. 我们可以 骑共享单车 去。

开车
骑自行车
坐出租车

3. 共享单车 怎么用？

手机
电脑
微信（Wēixìn，WeChat）

四、选词填空 Use the following words to fill in the blanks

> 开　骑　怎么　没事儿　教

1. 哪位老师_____你们汉语？

2. 你会_____车吗？

3. _____自行车去爬山很方便。

4. _____，我去问问别人吧。

5. 我不知道你的手机_____用。

五、根据课文内容回答问题 Answer the following questions according to the text

1. 王晨的哥哥为什么不能去爬山？

2. 马大为想怎么去？

3. 王晨为什么不想坐出租车去？

4. 王晨想怎么去？

六、根据课文内容填空 Fill in the blanks according to the text

马大为想和王晨一起去_____。王晨的哥哥有车，可是他下午有_____，不能去。马大为想坐_____去，王晨想骑_____去，_____马大为没有自行车。王晨说他们可以_____共享单车，马大为不知道_____用共享单车，王晨说很_____，他可以_____马大为。

七、汉字书写 Write Chinese characters

晴	日 + 青											
	丨	冂	日	日	日⁻	日=	旪	晴	晴	晴	晴	
爬	爪 + 巴											
	ノ	厂	爫	爪	爬	爬	爬	爬				
山	丨	山	山									
骑	马 + 奇											
	乛	马	马	马	驴	驴	骑	骑	骑	骑		
简	竹 + 间											
	ノ	⺮	⺮	⺮	竹	竹	竹	笱	筲	简	简	简
单	⺌ + 甲											
	丶	⺌	⺍	兴	兴	甾	单	单				

课文（二）
Text (Ⅱ)

(Ma Dawei and Wang Chen are climbing the mountain.)

Mǎ Dàwéi: Shān shàng de shùyè dōu hóng le, zhēn piàoliang a! Wáng Chén, nǐ kuài yìdiǎnr!
马大为：山上的树叶都红了，真漂亮啊！王晨，你快一点儿！

Wáng Chén: Nǐ pá de tài kuài le, děngdeng wǒ, wǒ lèi le.
王晨：你爬得太快了，等等我，我累了。

Mǎ Dàwéi: Jiāyóu! Jiāyóu!
马大为：加油！加油！

Wáng Chén: Nǐ shì bu shì cháng yùndòng?
王晨：你是不是常运动？

Mǎ Dàwéi: Duì, wǒ hěn ài yùndòng. Nǐ ne?
马大为：对，我很爱运动。你呢？

Wáng Chén: Wǒ měi tiān dōu xiǎng qù yùndòng.
王晨：我每天都想去运动。

Mǎ Dàwéi: Kěshì nǐ měi tiān dōu bú qù, duì bu duì?
马大为：可是你每天都不去，对不对？

Wáng Chén: Shì de.
王晨：是的。

Mǎ Dàwéi: Míngtiān nǐ hé wǒ yìqǐ qù pǎobù ba.
马大为：明天你和我一起去跑步吧。

Wáng Chén: Míngtiān yīntiān, kěnéng huì xià yǔ.
王晨：明天阴天，可能会下雨。

Mǎ Dàwéi: Méi guānxi, wǒmen kěyǐ qù jiànshēnfáng.
马大为：没关系，我们可以去健身房。

Ma Dawei: The leaves on the top of the mountain are all red. How beautiful! Wang Chen, hurry up!

Wang Chen: You climb too fast. Wait for me. I am tired.

Ma Dawei: Come on! Come on!

Wang Chen: Do you often take exercise?

Ma Dawei: Yeah, I love sports. How about you?

Wang Chen: I want to exercise everyday.

Ma Dawei: But you don't do it every day, right?

Wang Chen: Yes.

Ma Dawei: You can run with me tomorrow.

Wang Chen: It is cloudy tomorrow. It may rain.

Ma Dawei: It's doesn't matter. We can go to the gym.

生词 New words

1. 树叶	shùyè	n.	leaf
2. 漂亮	piàoliang	adj.	beautiful
3. 快	kuài	adj.	fast
4. 一点儿	yìdiǎnr	num.-m.	a little
5. 等	děng	v.	to wait
6. 累	lèi	adj.	tired
7. 加油	jiāyóu	v.	to make an extra effort, to come on
8. 运动	yùndòng	v.	to take exercise
9. 爱	ài	v.	to love
10. 每天	měi tiān		every day
11. 跑步	pǎobù	v.	to run
12. 阴天	yīntiān	n.	overcast sky, cloudy day
13. 会	huì	mod.v.	to be likely to
14. 下雨	xià yǔ	VO	to rain
下	xià	v.	to (of rain, snow, etc.) fall
雨	yǔ	n.	rain
15. 健身房	jiànshēnfáng	n.	gym
健身	jiànshēn	v.	to keep fit

语言点 Language Points

一、数量词"一点儿" Numeral measure word "一点儿"

数量词"一点儿"可以用在名词的前边，表示数量很少。例如：

The numeral measure word "一点儿" can be used before nouns to indicate a small amount. For example:

1. 我吃了一点儿面包。

2. 今天下了一点儿雨。

"一点儿"也可以用在形容词的后边，表示程度，意思是"略微"。例如：

"一点儿" can also be used after an adjective to express the degree, which is slight. For example:

3. 王晨，你快一点儿！

4. 黄裙子好看一点儿。

5. 我的眼睛好一点儿了。

注意："一"可以省略。

Attention: "一" can be omitted.

6. 你好点儿了吗？

※ 练习：请用数量词"一点儿"回答问题 Please answer the questions with numeral measure word "一点儿"

1. 你想吃什么？
   _____。

2. 你想买什么？
   _____。

3. 马大为和金龙，谁跑得快？
   _____。

二、能愿动词"会"（2） Modal verb "会" (2)

能愿动词"会"，可以表示事情发生的可能性，否定形式为"不会"。例如：

The modal verb "会" can express the possibility of something happening. The negative form is "不会". For example:

1. 明天阴天，可能会下雨。
2. 美丽明天会来你家玩儿吗？
3. 马大为今天肚子疼，他不会来踢足球了。

※ 练习：请用能愿动词"会"和所给词语完成句子　Please complete sentences with modal verb "会" and the given words

1. 马大为今天早上说眼睛很疼，他＿＿＿＿＿＿＿＿＿＿＿＿＿＿。（看电影）
2. 今天下雨，王晨＿＿＿＿＿＿＿＿＿＿＿＿＿＿＿＿＿。（爬山）
3. 李真很忙，她今天＿＿＿＿＿＿＿＿＿＿＿＿＿＿＿＿。（去健身）
4. 他病（fall ill）了，今天＿＿＿＿＿＿＿＿＿＿＿＿＿＿＿。（上课）

综合练习 Comprehensive Exercises

一、根据汉字写拼音　Write Pinyin according to Chinese characters

1. 树叶＿＿＿＿＿　　3. 运动＿＿＿＿＿　　5. 跑步＿＿＿＿＿
2. 漂亮＿＿＿＿＿　　4. 下雨＿＿＿＿＿　　6. 阴天＿＿＿＿＿

二、朗读语句　Read aloud

1. 快一点儿
2. 等一下
3. 有点儿累
4. 山上的树叶真漂亮。
5. 我很爱运动。
6. 明天一起去跑步吧。

三、替换练习 Substitution drills

1. <u>山上的树叶</u> 都 <u>红</u> 了。

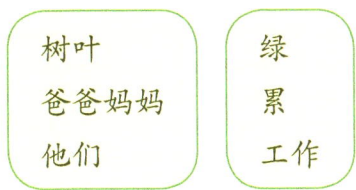

2. <u>快</u> 一点儿 <u>爬</u>！

3. 明天可能会 <u>下雨</u>。

去爬山
去北京
和朋友去吃饭

四、选词填空 Use the following words to fill in the blanks

1. 我不_____吃米饭，你呢？

2. 树叶都黄_____，天气也冷了。

3. 明天可能_____下雨。

4. 你爬得太快了，_____我一下。

5. 你的眼睛好_____了吗？

五、根据课文内容回答问题 Answer the following questions according to the text

1. 谁爬山爬得快?

2. 马大为常运动吗?

3. 王晨常运动吗?

4. 马大为明天想做什么?

六、根据课文内容填空 Fill in the blanks according to the text

王晨和马大为一起去_____。山上的树叶都红_____，很_____。王晨叫(to ask)马大为不要爬_____太快了，_____他。马大为很_____运动，也_____运动。王晨每天都想去运动，_____他每天都不去。

七、汉字书写 Write Chinese characters

漂	氵+票	丶	丶	氵	氵	汀	沪	洒	洒	漂	漂	漂	漂
亮	亠+几	丶	亠	宀	亡	吉	吉	亨	亭	亮			
等	竹+寺	丿	卜	厃	朴	竹	竹	竺	竺	笙	笙	等	等
累	田+糸	丨	冂	冃	用	田	田	胃	胃	累	累		
爱	爫+友	丶	丷	爫	爫	爫	爫	严	孚	爱	爱		
雨		一	厂	冂	雨	雨	雨	雨	雨				

语言任务 Language Tasks

一、阅读理解 Reading comprehension

今天马大为和王晨一起骑共享单车去爬山了。山上的树叶都红了，非常漂亮。马大为爬得很快，他很爱运动，每天都跑步，阴天下雨的时候也去健身房运动。王晨不太喜欢运动，觉得（juéde, to think）爬山非常累。

读后判断 True or false

1. 山上很漂亮。   （   ）
2. 马大为和王晨都喜欢运动。   （   ）
3. 马大为和王晨坐出租车去爬山了。   （   ）

二、口头表达 Oral expression

任务名称：我们去爬山吧。

Task: Let's go climbing.

任务要求：1. 两名学生一组，一起去爬山。

2. 一起商量出行方式，并约定以后一起多运动。

Requirements: 1. Work in the group of two and go climbing together.

2. Discuss travel methods together and reach the agreement of having more exercise together hereafter.

Reference words: 骑　共享单车　出租车　跑步　健身房　了　一点儿　爱　累

第十五课　天晴了
Lesson 15　The sky clears up

词汇总表
Glossary

			A	
啊	a	*part.*	a modal particle used at the end of a sentence to express affirmation	4
爱	ài	*v.*	to love	15
			B	
八	bā	*num.*	eight	5
爸爸	bàba	*n.*	father, dad	4
吧	ba	*part.*	used at the end of a sentence to indicate a mild suggestion	6
白大褂	báidàguà	*n.*	white coat	14
百	bǎi	*num.*	hundred	5
办公室	bàngōngshì	*n.*	office	13
半	bàn	*num.*	half	7
杯子	bēizi	*n.*	cup	14
北京烤鸭	Běijīng kǎoyā		Beijing Roast Duck	12
笔记本	bǐjìběn	*n.*	notebook	14
别的	biéde	*pron.*	other	8
别人	biérén	*pron.*	someone else	11
病人	bìngrén	*n.*	patient	13
不错	búcuò	*adj.*	good, not bad	14
不客气	bú kèqi		you are welcome	8
不用	búyòng	*adv.*	need not	13
不	bù	*adv.*	no, not	1
不好意思	bù hǎoyìsi		sorry	11

216

不行	bùxíng		v.	to be not allowed	13
		C			
菜	cài		n.	dish	12
茶	chá		n.	tea	12
差	chà		v.	to be short of	7
常	cháng		adv.	often, usually	12
车	chē		n.	car	15
吃	chī		v.	to eat	6
吃饭	chīfàn		v.	to have a meal	6
抽	chōu		v.	to smoke	13
抽烟	chōuyān		v.	to smoke (a cigarette or a pipe)	13
出租车	chūzūchē		n.	taxi	15
穿	chuān		v.	to wear	14
床	chuáng		n.	bed	10
		D			
打	dǎ		v.	to dial	11
打电话	dǎ diànhuà		VO	to make a call	11
大	dà		adj.	old, big	6
大号	dàhào		adj.	large-size	14
单车	dānchē		n.	bike	15
当然	dāngrán		adv.	of course, certainly	8
到	dào		v.	to arrive	7
的	de		part.	used to indicate a possessive relationship	3
得	de		part.	a structural particle, used after verbs or adjectives to connect complements of degree and result	12
等	děng		v.	to wait	15
地方	dìfang		n.	place	11
点	diǎn		m.	o'clock	7
点	diǎn		v.	to order dishes	12
电话	diànhuà		n.	phone	5
电脑	diànnǎo		n.	computer	7
电视	diànshì		n.	television	10

电影	diànyǐng	n.	movie	9
订	dìng	v.	to order	12
订外卖	dìng wàimài	VO	to order a takeaway	12
东	dōng	n.	east	11
东边	dōngbian	n.	east	11
东西	dōngxi	n.	thing	13
都	dōu	adv.	both, all	3
读	dú	v.	to read	7
读书	dúshū	v.	to read, to study	7
肚子	dùzi	n.	abdomen	12
对	duì	adj.	right	3
对不起	duìbuqǐ	v.	I'm sorry; excuse me	1
多	duō	adj.	many, much	4
多	duō	pron.	used to ask degree or quantity in interrogative sentences	6
多少	duōshao	pron.	how many, how much	5

E

二	èr	num.	two	6
二十一	èrshíyī	num.	twenty-one	6

F

饭	fàn	n.	meal	6
饭店	fàndiàn	n.	restaurant	12
方便	fāngbiàn	adj.	convenient	10
房间	fángjiān	n.	room	9
非常	fēicháng	adv.	very, extremely	5
分	fēn	m.	minute	7
分钟	fēnzhōng	m.	minute	10
服务员	fúwùyuán	n.	waiter, waitress	12

G

高兴	gāoxìng	adj.	happy, glad	2
哥哥	gēge	n.	elder brother	9

个	gè	m.	a measure word used before nouns without a special classifier of their own	5
给	gěi	prep.	to, for	11
工作	gōngzuò	v./n.	to work; job	9
公共	gōnggòng	adj.	public, common	10
公共汽车	gōnggòng qìchē		bus	10
宫保鸡丁	gōngbǎo jīdīng		spicy diced chicken, Kung Pao chicken	12
共享	gòngxiǎng	v.	to share	15
共享单车	gòngxiǎng dānchē		shared bike	15
狗	gǒu	n.	dog	4
贵	guì		your (used to modify things of the other part of the conversation to show respect)	2
贵	guì	adj.	expensive	8
贵姓	guìxìng	n.	(your honorable) surname	2
国	guó	n.	country	3
过	guò	v.	to spend (time)	6

H

还	hái	adv.	in addition, also, still	8
还是	háishi	conj.	or	11
好	hǎo	adj.	good, well, fine	1
好	hǎo	adj.	used to express approval or agreement	6
好吃	hǎochī	adj.	delicious	12
好看	hǎokàn	adj.	beautiful, good-looking	14
号	hào	m.	date	6
号码	hàomǎ	n.	number	5
喝	hē	v.	to drink	12
和	hé	conj.	and, with	4
黑	hēi	adj.	black	14
黑色	hēisè	n.	black	14
很	hěn	adv.	very	2
红	hóng	adj.	red	14
红色	hóngsè	n.	red	14

词汇总表
Glossary

后	hòu		n.	behind, back	11
后面	hòumiàn		n.	behind	11
护士	hùshi		n.	nurse	6
花园	huāyuán		n.	garden	11
黄	huáng		adj.	yellow	14
黄色	huángsè		n.	yellow	14
会	huì		mod.v.	can, to be able to	12
会	huì		mod.v.	to be likely to	15
		J			
几	jǐ		pron.	how many	4
加油	jiāyóu		v.	to make an extra effort, to come on	15
家	jiā		n.	home, family	4
家属	jiāshǔ		n.	family member	13
家庭	jiātíng		n.	family	9
简单	jiǎndān		adj.	easy, simple	15
见	jiàn		v.	to see, to meet	10
件	jiàn		m.	piece	14
健身	jiànshēn		v.	to keep fit	15
健身房	jiànshēnfáng		n.	gym	15
教	jiāo		v.	to teach	15
角	jiǎo		m.	*jiao*, a fractional unit of money in China, 1/10 of a *yuan*	14
叫	jiào		v.	to be called	2
教室	jiàoshì		n.	classroom	7
教学	jiàoxué		v.	to teach	11
教学楼	jiàoxuélóu		n.	teaching building	11
节	jié		n.	festival	6
节日	jiérì		n.	festival	6
解剖	jiěpōu		v.	to dissect	11
解剖楼	jiěpōulóu		n.	anatomy building	11
斤	jīn		m.	*jin*, a unit of weight, equivalent to 500g	8
今年	jīnnián		n.	this year	6

今天	jīntiān	*n.*	today	6
近	jìn	*adj.*	near	10
九	jiǔ	*num.*	nine	5
旧	jiù	*adj.*	old	14
就	jiù	*adv.*	as early as	7
就	jiù	*adv.*	exactly, precisely	11

K

开	kāi	*v.*	to drive, to operate	15
开车	kāichē	*v.*	to drive	15
看	kàn	*v.*	to see, to watch, to treat (a patient or an illness)	9
看电影	kàn diànyǐng	*VO*	to see a movie	9
可能	kěnéng	*mod.v.*	perhaps, maybe, probably	5
可是	kěshì	*conj.*	but, however	11
可以	kěyǐ	*mod.v.*	may, can	8
刻	kè	*m.*	quarter	7
课	kè	*n.*	class, lesson	7
口	kǒu	*m.*	a measure word for family members, etc.	4
块	kuài	*m.*	*yuan*, the basic currency unit in China	8
快	kuài	*adj.*	fast	15

L

来	lái	*v.*	to come	10
阑尾炎	lánwěiyán	*n.*	appendicitis	13
蓝	lán	*adj.*	blue	14
蓝色	lánsè	*n.*	blue	14
老师	lǎoshī	*n.*	teacher	1
了	le	*part.*	an aspectual particle to indicate the completion of an action	12
累	lèi	*adj.*	tired	15
冷	lěng	*adj.*	cold	6
离	lí	*v.*	to be away from	10
里	lǐ	*n.*	inside	10
里边	lǐbian	*n.*	inside, within, in	10

词汇总表
Glossary

里面	lǐmiàn	n.	inside	11
两	liǎng	num.	two	5
留学	liúxué	v.	to study abroad	1
留学生	liúxuéshēng	n.	international student	1
六	liù	num.	six	5
楼	lóu	n.	building	11
路	lù	n.	route	10
绿	lǜ	adj.	green	14
绿色	lǜsè	n.	green	14
M				
妈妈	māma	n.	mother, mom	4
马上	mǎshàng	adv.	immediately	13
吗	ma	part.	used at the end of a sentence to indicate a question	1
买	mǎi	v.	to buy	8
忙	máng	adj.	busy	9
猫	māo	n.	cat	4
毛	máo	m.	mao, a fractional unit of money in China, ten cents	8
没关系	méi guānxi	VO	it doesn't matter; it's OK	1
没事儿	méishìr	v.	it doesn't matter; that's all right	15
没有	méiyǒu	v.	there is not; to not have	4
每	měi	pron.	each, every	10
每个	měi gè		each of	10
每天	měi tiān		every day	15
门	mén	n.	entrance, gate, door	10
们	men	suf.	used after a personal pronoun or a noun to show plural number	2
米饭	mǐfàn	n.	cooked rice	12
面包	miànbāo	n.	bread	8
名字	míngzi	n.	name	2
明天	míngtiān	n.	tomorrow	7
N				
哪	nǎ	pron.	which	3

哪儿	nǎr	pron.	where	9
那	nà	pron.	that	3
那些	nàxiē	pron.	those	3
南	nán	n.	south	10
南门	nánmén	n.	south gate	10
呢	ne	part.	marker of a special, alternative or rhetorical question	2
能	néng	mod.v.	can	13
你	nǐ	pron.	you	1
你们	nǐmen	pron.	you (plural)	2
年	nián	n.	year	6
您	nín	pron.	you, respectful form of	2
P				
爬	pá	v.	to climb	15
爬山	pá shān	VO	to climb mountains	15
旁边	pángbiān	n.	beside	12
跑步	pǎobù	v.	to run	15
朋友	péngyou	n.	friend	3
漂亮	piàoliang	adj.	beautiful	15
苹果	píngguǒ	n.	apple	8
瓶	píng	m./n.	a bottle of; bottle	8
Q				
七	qī	num.	seven	6
骑	qí	v.	to ride	15
起床	qǐchuáng	v.	to get up	7
汽车	qìchē	n.	automobile, car	10
千	qiān	num.	thousand	5
前	qián	n.	before	7
前面	qiánmiàn	n.	ahead	11
钱	qián	n.	money	8
晴	qíng	adj.	sunny, clear	15
请	qǐng	v.	please	2

请客	qǐngkè	v.	to treat, to invite sb. to dinner		12
请问	qǐngwèn	v.	excuse me, please		2
去	qù	v.	to go		9
裙子	qúnzi	n.	skirt		14
		R			
热	rè	adj.	hot		6
人	rén	n.	person		3
认识	rènshi	v.	to know		2
日	rì		a certain day		6
日	rì	n.	day		6
		S			
三	sān	num.	three		4
山	shān	n.	mountain		15
上	shàng	n.	up, upward		14
上课	shàngkè	v.	to go to class		7
上午	shàngwǔ	n.	morning		9
少	shǎo	adj.	less, few		14
谁	shéi	pron.	who		3
什么	shénme	pron.	what		2
生日	shēngrì	n.	birthday		6
十	shí	num.	ten		6
十二	shí'èr	num.	twelve		6
时候	shíhou	n.	time		6
时间	shíjiān	n.	time		9
实验	shíyàn	n./v.	experiment; to test		11
实验楼	shíyànlóu	n.	the laboratory building		11
是	shì	v.	to be, is/am/are		1
手机	shǒujī	n.	cellphone		5
手术	shǒushù	n.	operation		13
售货员	shòuhuòyuán	n.	shop assistant		8
书	shū	n.	book		3

书包	shūbāo	n.	bag	14
树叶	shùyè	n.	leaf	15
水	shuǐ	n.	water	8
水果	shuǐguǒ	n.	fruit	8
睡觉	shuìjiào	v.	to go to bed	7
说	shuō	v.	to say	9
四	sì	num.	four	6
宿舍	sùshè	n.	dormitory	5
岁	suì	m.	year (of age)	6
		T		
他	tā	pron.	he, him	3
他们	tāmen	pron.	they, them	4
她	tā	pron.	she	3
太	tài	adv.	extremely	7
太……了	tài…le		too, extremely	7
疼	téng	adj.	painful, aching	9
踢	tī	v.	to kick	12
踢足球	tī zúqiú	VO	to play football	12
天	tiān	m.	day	6
天	tiān	n.	sky, weather	6
天气	tiānqì	n.	weather	6
条	tiáo	m.	a measure word for slender things	14
同学	tóngxué	n.	classmate	4
图书馆	túshūguǎn	n.	library	11
		W		
外	wài	n.	out	11
外国	wàiguó	n.	foreign country	4
外卖	wàimài	n.	take-out, takeaway	12
外面	wàimiàn	n.	outside	11
玩儿	wánr	v.	to play	7
晚	wǎn	adj.	late	7

晚上	wǎnshang	n.	evening		9
碗	wǎn	n.	bowl		12
卫生间	wèishēngjiān	n.	bathroom		13
为什么	wèi shénme		why		7
位	wèi	m.	a measure word for people with respect		12
喂	wèi	int.	hello		9
问	wèn	v.	to ask		2
我	wǒ	pron.	I, me		1
我们	wǒmen	pron.	we, us		3
五	wǔ	num.	five		5
		X			
喜欢	xǐhuan	v.	to like		5
下	xià	v.	to (of rain, snow, etc.) fall		15
下课	xiàkè	v.	to finish class		7
下午	xiàwǔ	n.	afternoon		7
下雨	xià yǔ	VO	to rain		15
先生	xiānsheng	n.	Mr, sir		12
现在	xiànzài	n.	now		7
想	xiǎng	v.	to miss		4
想	xiǎng	v.	to want to, to would like to		8
小	xiǎo	adj.	small		13
小号	xiǎohào	adj.	small size		14
小区	xiǎoqū	n.	community		10
写	xiě	v.	to write		7
谢谢	xièxie	v.	to thank		8
新	xīn	adj.	new		14
星期	xīngqī	n.	week		7
星期六	xīngqīliù	n.	Saturday		7
行	xíng	v.	to be all right		13
幸福	xìngfú	adj.	happy		10
姓	xìng	n./v.	family name, surname; one's surname is		2

休息	xiūxi	v.	to rest	9
学生	xuésheng	n.	student	1
学习	xuéxí	v.	to study	4
学校	xuéxiào	n.	school	10
学院	xuéyuàn	n.	college, academy	5

Y

呀	ya	part.	a modal particle used at the end of a sentence to express affirmation, like	5
烟	yān	n.	tobacco, cigarette	13
颜色	yánsè	n.	color	14
眼睛	yǎnjing	n.	eye	9
要	yào	v.	to want, to ask for	8
要	yào	mod.v.	must, should	13
也	yě	adv.	too, also	2
一	yī	num.	one	6
衣服	yīfu	n.	clothes	14
医生	yīshēng	n.	doctor	9
医学院	yīxuéyuàn	n.	medical school	5
医院	yīyuàn	n.	hospital	9
一定	yídìng	adv.	must	14
一共	yígòng	adv.	altogether, in total	8
一下	yíxià	num.-m.	once	13
以后	yǐhòu	n.	after	13
椅子	yǐzi	n.	chair	10
一点儿	yìdiǎnr	num.-m.	a little	15
一起	yìqǐ	adv.	together	4
一直	yìzhí	adv.	continuously, always	9
意思	yìsi	n.	meaning	11
阴天	yīntiān	n.	overcast sky, cloudy day	15
用	yòng	v.	to need	13
用	yòng	v.	to use	15
游戏	yóuxì	n.	game	7

有	yǒu	v.	to have	4
有点儿	yǒudiǎnr	adv.	a little bit	12
右	yòu	n.	right	11
右边	yòubian	n.	rightside	11
雨	yǔ	n.	rain	15
远	yuǎn	adj.	far	10
月	yuè	n.	month	6
运动	yùndòng	v.	to take exercise	15
		Z		
再见	zàijiàn	v.	see you; goodbye	1
在	zài	prep./v.	in, at; to stay	9
早	zǎo	n./adj.	morning; early	7
早饭	zǎofàn	n.	breakfast	13
早上	zǎoshang	n.	morning	7
怎么	zěnme	pron.	how	15
怎么样	zěnmeyàng	pron.	how about	10
站	zhàn	n.	station	10
这	zhè	pron.		3
这儿	zhèr	pron.	here	13
这些	zhèxiē	pron.	these	14
真	zhēn	adv./adj.	really; real	4
支付	zhīfù	v.	to pay	8
知道	zhīdào	v.	to know, to be aware of	11
中午	zhōngwǔ	n.	noon	7
种	zhǒng	m.	kind, sort	14
重要	zhòngyào	adj.	important	6
主妇	zhǔfù	n.	housewife	9
住	zhù	v.	to live, to reside	10
准备	zhǔnbèi	v.	to prepare	13
桌子	zhuōzi	n.	table	10
自行车	zìxíngchē	n.	bike	15

字	zì		n.	handwriting	14
足球	zúqiú		n.	football	12
最	zuì		adv.	most	9
昨天	zuótiān		n.	yesterday	9
左	zuǒ		n.	left	11
左边	zuǒbian		n.	leftside	11
作业	zuòyè		n.	homework	7
坐	zuò		v.	to take	10
做	zuò		v.	to do	7
做	zuò		v.	to cook	12
做饭	zuòfàn		v.	to cook, to prepare a meal	12
做手术	zuò shǒushù		VO	to have an operation	13

专名 Proper nouns

B			
北京	Běijīng	Beijing	12
F			
法国	Fǎguó	France	4
H			
韩国	Hánguó	Korea	4
汉语	Hànyǔ	Chinese	8
护士节	Hùshi Jié	Nurses' Day	6
J			
金龙	Jīn Lóng	name of a Thai student	1
L			
李真	Lǐ Zhēn	name of a Chinese student	2
M			
马大为	Mǎ Dàwéi	name of a Nepalese student	2
美国	Měiguó	America	4
美丽	Měilì	name of a South African student	1
N			
南非	Nánfēi	South Africa	3

尼泊尔	Níbó'ěr	Nepal	3
T			
泰国	Tàiguó	Thailand	3
W			
王	Wáng	a surname in Chinese	1
王晨	Wáng Chén	name of a Chinese student	1
王东	Wáng Dōng	name of a Chinese doctor, Wang Chen's elder brother	12
X			
幸福小区	Xìngfú Xiǎoqū	the Happiness Community	10
Y			
元旦	Yuándàn	New Year's Day	6
月亮	Yuèliang	name of a Bahraini student	4
Z			
中国	Zhōngguó	China	3